FOREWORD BY PIYUSH PANDEY:
"Go ahead and blow up some good money on branded content or else read this book carefully!"

BRANDED CONTENT BOSS

Featuring Case Studies & Examples from Apple, BMW, Coke, Dove, Lego, Nike, P&G, Red Bull, Amul, Ching's, Maruti, MTV & more.

BRANDED CONTENT BOSS

ASHIISH V PATIL

Bigfoot Publications
Because, there's a writer in everyone.

Branded Content Boss!
Author : Ashiish V Patil

First Published by
Bigfoot06 Publications (OPC) Pvt. Ltd.
1st floor, BSR Building near Vishal Mega Mart,
Daultabad Flyover, Laxman Vihar Phase 3,
Gurugram, Haryana (122001)
Website: www.bigfootpublications.in
Email: info@bigfootpublications.in

First Edition : February, 2024

ISBN Print Book : **978-81-970347-5-6**

Printed in India.

To the ones who taught me how to tell a story.
And the ones who paid me to do that.

FOREWORD | PIYUSH PANDEY

Branded Content is perhaps the most misused tool by those who sell it and the least understood by those who buy it.

If it is good content like a good movie or a serial, one becomes an advertiser on it at best. Or one becomes a lead sponsor like Binaca did for a music programme or Bournvita for a quiz contest. This certainly in my mind is not Branded Content.

Branded Content is when a brand plays an active part in the content, like Aston Martin did in James Bond films for years. In the recent past, Coke has done a great job by truly partnering music creators and building an iconic content property in Coke Studio.

Don't expect annual sales to rise on the back of this 'branded content'.

But if you want to have a meaningful emotional connection with the brand's audience through culture or be seen as a good citizen then go ahead and be one without any short-term sales illusion.

This book will give you enough fodder to think and make up your mind – what does Formula 1 do to car brands, what do World Cups do to the brands who 'sponsor it'.

Does dancing and singing songs with a soap brand's poster in the background mean branded content? Are all these marketing devices just an excuse to hobnob with celebrities at these events?

If you don't agree with me, go ahead and blow up some good money on branded content or else read this book carefully before making up your mind.

PREFACE

Picture yourself as a tiny, enthusiastic sperm swimming among millions in the race for that elusive egg – consumer attention. It's a battlefield out there and it's brutal. You've got some serious competition. It's not just the clutter and gutter of marketing and advertising messages but also the heavy-hitter superstars with their blockbuster movies, chartbuster songs and gut-buster sports events that you're up against. But fear not! Branded Content is your secret weapon.

I still remember the time when I was in advertising and 'digital' used to be presented as a 'media innovation'. And that meant a banner on Rediff.com! Digital today is no longer essential for success, but needed for survival. Branded Content is the same now. Global advertising spends are upwards of US$ 600 billion, and Content Marketing/ Branded Content is under US$ 80 billion according to some estimates. But Branded Content is growing at twice the pace of traditional advertising!

You see, just like building a romantic relationship, branded content is all about trust, baby! It's more than the charming grin, the cheeky smile, the smart pick-up line. You start with a spark, a captivating story, a hilarious video or a jaw-dropping experience that grabs their attention. And as the relationship progresses, you keep the fire burning. Planning date nights, wining, dining and surprising with compelling content. Consistently. Delivering value, entertainment and a sense of authenticity. Like sending flowers, cooking their favorite meal, little things that say, "Hey, I'm invested in this relationship."

The 'fertilization' of the egg is not the end goal as a one-time conversion. No, no, no. We're in it for the long haul. It's the moment when you go from being just another fish in the sea to their one and only. The ultimate climax – a devoted, passionate audience that sticks with you through thick and thin.

Cue dashing exit with a wink and nod ;)

THANK YOU

To all you incredible clients, agencies, platforms and partners out there who've had the vision and the balls to punt on content and trust me to create it for you.

To all the creative mavericks I've been lucky enough to have got a chance to work with – you know who you are. I've learned so damn much from each and every one of you. This book is my attempt to bring some structure to those lessons and pass them forward. We've made our fair share of mistakes, but hey, that's how we grow. I hope this book helps others avoid those pitfalls, and, who knows maybe even make some new ones that take all our learning to the next level.

And to you, the readers, who've picked up this book. You're the reason I poured my blood, sweat, tears and some other bodily fluids into these pages. So, if some of the pages are a bit smudged, you know why.

Life is full of certainties like death, change and taxes interrupted by commercial breaks. But if you truly want to thrive, you need one more thing: a permanent learner's license. The world of Marketing and Entertainment moves faster than a cheetah on Red Bull. Just when you think you've got it all figured out, some fresh-faced genius will pop up and teach you kung fu again. So never stop learning. Never stop being a trainee, eager to soak up every bit of knowledge that comes your way.

That, my friends, is the only true secret to becoming a boss at anything.

And last but not the least, to the best content of my life, my son Risshan. Rissh is on the autism spectrum and shows me how to be a better dad, a better content creator and a better person every day. A part of the proceeds from this book goes to a Centre for Autism and other Developmental Differences

Thank you, from the bottom of my heart and the heart of my bottom.

WHO IS THIS FOR?

If you're ready to take your game to the next level and become a Branded Content Boss, then this book is for you. Meant for a diverse range of people who are ready to take, both the marketing and entertainment world by storm!

1. **Advertising/ Marketing/ Communication Folks:**

First up, we've got the marketing and advertising professionals. The challenge with traditional marketing thinking and advertising agencies is just that. Being traditional. Hacking and cracking Branded Content is an essential life-skill to survive in today's world. Filled to the brim with insights and strategies that will help you connect with your audience like never before and not just think beyond the traditional '30 second spot', 'hoarding layout' and 'radio jingle' but also serve as a practical guide on how to do that.

2. **Content Creators:**

Now, let's not forget the writers, film-makers, influencers, producers, directors, musicians, singers, artists, influencers who bring stories to life. Just the way brands can no longer afford to interrupt a consumer's experience to grab attention, they don't have to be integrated into your content by disrupting it either. Done smartly, it can even enhance the experience and impact. Additionally, supplement income, help you build reach by amplifying your message and even add to your credibility. After all, being profitable gives you the privilege to be creative. If you hope to do this without sacrificing your authenticity, this book is your secret weapon. It can help you crack how to partner with brands to seamlessly integrate them into content, to create fresh content that delivers not just on their marketing objectives but also still engages audiences. In short, do what you like to do and get paid for it!

3. Brand Managers and Executives:

Next on the list are the teams at a Company responsible to ensure that the brand continues to buzz, excite, engage with its consumers in the most relevant manner. The teams tasked to work with agencies, creators and creative mavericks to co-create content, messaging and marketing plans and deliver them with impact. This book will equip you with the knowledge needed to navigate the ever-changing landscape of Branded Content. It will serve as a tool to help you up your game. To write briefs that inspire and extract the best work from creative partners, to help you evaluate them to ensure the work is in line with brand objectives and create memorable content that works. So, say goodbye to outdated strategies and hello to innovative approaches that will make your brand shine brighter than ever.

4. Students and Aspiring Professionals:

If you're hungry to start out your career in advertising, marketing, or content creation, this book is for you too! It's a GPS to your ultimate destination. Packed with insider tips, industry secrets and real-world advice to help you kickstart your journey, it will also give you an edge over competition. Get ready to turn your passion into a profession.

5. Curious Cats:

Last but not the least, we've got everyone else. Yep, that means you too! Maybe you're just curious about the latest trends and best practices in the world of marketing, branded entertainment content. Well, this book is your front-row seat to the cutting-edge strategies, the mind-blowing campaigns, and the jaw-dropping innovations that are shaping the industry. So, if you want to be in the know, sit back and soak it in!

TABLE OF CONTENTS

WHAT THE HELL IS THIS BRANDED CONTENT?

Viral video featuring BBC News Anchor Zoom-crashed during a live telecast by his kids and their nanny

We all hate being interrupted, whether it's during a date, a casual hangout with friends, or even a work presentation. But here's the thing: traditional advertising and marketing have always thrived on interruption. They disrupt your favorite show, the news, an event, a crucial moment or break the momentum of whatever was going on.

For most, it's the cue for a loo break. To go grab the popcorn or to switch channels. And let's face it, most of us have become ninjas at skipping ads or using ad blockers. One button to bypass an entire industry! People are even spending real money to not have to see ads. Even those sneaky product placements in content have started to go unnoticed. Can you even remember the brand on your favorite athlete's jersey? If not disruptive, its passive, my friends!

But the entertainment industry cracked the code. They discovered the secret sauce. You see, movies have long used entertainment content to market their product which is also entertainment content. But there's one key difference – this is entertainment content that we actually *want* to consume. Think about it: the trailers, the badass posters, the killer songs, the music videos, or when the cast appears on a talk show like Kapil Sharma in India or Fallon and Kimmel internationally. PVR Cinemas even has a paid show where you can watch trailers back-to-back on the big screen. Take my money already!

Marvel's Avengers franchise... the most successful film franchise of all time with over 22+ films clocking more than US$ 22 billion globally

Every piece of entertainment content hypes us up, piques our curiosity, and gets us excited enough to fork over our hard-earned money for the end product. And if the movie is damn good, it holds us hostage until the end credits roll. That's when a bond forms. And we're willing to shell out even more money to watch the prequel/ sequel/ spin-off, binge the series, buy the t-shirt, eat the meal, ride the ride, play the game.

Now, some brilliant minds thought, *"Hey, why not blend entertainment content with marketing messages until you can't tell them apart?"* And just like that, Branded Content was born – the beautiful love child of Advertising/ Marketing and Entertainment.

So, what exactly is Branded Content?

"Branded Content is content created by a brand to entertain, engage and inform its target audience while [subtly] promoting its products or services. This can take many form, from short films, songs, music videos, web series to books, events, feature films, blogs, and more."

But here's the kicker – this kind of advertising doesn't interrupt or disrupt. It's the kind of advertising people actually search for. It doesn't need to buy time or space to play/ publish. It earns its own media. It's the advertising that people *don't* want to block or skip. And guess what? It's a wise financial and time investment for brands and audiences. Its entertainment created by brands themselves.

That's where the difference lies. Traditional advertising is all about promoting products or services directly, often through interruptive methods like commercials, billboards, or annoying pop-up ads. But Branded Content's primary goal isn't to sell directly. It's about engaging the audience, building that deep emotional connection, and fostering a positive brand association by providing value and entertainment.

There are mentions of a Chinese writer advertising his tobacco shop in informational flyers about medicine as way back as 1806 and even Charles Dickens used to barter railroad mentions in his writings in the 19th century to get a free ride.

1806, China

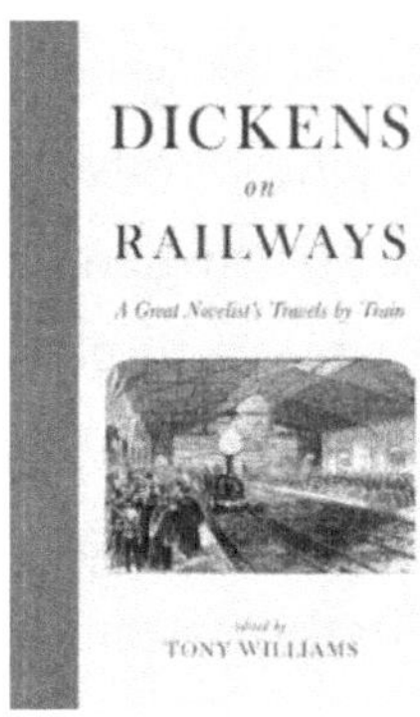

Dickens railroad barters in literature

Flashback: Procter and Gamble was one of the pioneers, creating radio programs in the 1930's and serialised shows on TV in the mid 1950's. 'As the World Turns' and 'The Edge of Night' were among the first half-hour shows to hit the CBS TV Network. P&G literally put the soap in soap opera. Even before Ekta Kapoor could. And they managed to do it minus any Ks in the title.

'As the World Turns', 1st ever soap-opera, produced by P&G, aired on CBS TV Network on Apr 2, 1956.

Among the first Indian branded shows was the cult, Binaca Geetmala, that was broadcast on Radio Ceylon from 1952 to 1988, and then shifted to the Vividh Bharati Service of All India Radio [AIR] where it ran until 1994. It was the first radio countdown show of Indian Film songs and since AIR had banned Hindi film music, it was being broadcast out of Sri Lanka. Hosted by the legendary Mr. Ameen Sayani – who still remains one of the most imitated hosts/ RJs – making his way even into a Varun Dhawan/ Alia Bhatt remix of Tamma Tamma. Binaca Top was a toothpaste brand owned by Reckitt's and the show was one of the early examples of brand integration even if the format was a simple sponsorship.

Ameen Sayani with the cult Radio show, 'Binaca Geetmala'

Then, back in the swinging 60's, when Amul wanted to promote their butter, they brought in ad legend, the late Sylvester DaCunha, to design an advertising campaign that would shake things up. And boy, did they hit it out of the park! They started putting up these epic hoardings with topical ads that tackled everyday issues, events, and happenings. They introduced the one and only Amul Girl who was first sketched by genius art director Eustace Fernandes.

Fast forward to today, and these ads are part of pop culture. You can't wait to see what Amul's take is going to be on the next big thing, whether it's an IPL win, an Oscar nod, or an Election victory.

Amul's 1st ever hoarding designed by DaCunha Associates in 1966

Now, let's talk about Content Marketing and Branded Content. They might sound similar, yes, they're related *but two distinct* concepts in the realm of advertising and marketing.

Content marketing is all about creating and sharing information or educational content designed to drive profitable customer action. We're talking about lead generation, sales, all that good stuff. On the other hand, Branded Content has a slightly softer agenda. It's all about building that brand association and loyalty. We're not just selling products here; we're creating an emotional bond.

Sure, content marketing might involve unboxing videos, FAQs, user manuals, guides, test drives, reviews, workshops, tutorials, white papers, reports, survey findings and a lot of content around the product, service. It's about providing potential customers with the information they need to make a decision or arming the sales team with the tools they need to seal the deal. But you know what? There's no rule saying we can't make all of these content assets entertaining as hell. We can go beyond the purely informative and educational stuff and really create that emotional connection. Because here's the secret – every brand touchpoint should look, sound, feel, smell, and taste like the brand itself.

When I was in advertising *[my scars are still fresh from it!]* at SSC&B Lintas, we used to service the Allwyn Refrigerators account. When they launched a super-premium, big-ass Frost Free refrigerator, we decided to up-end even the user-manual that went with it. So, we'd designed a 'Kitchen Manager's Guide', complete with tear-out planners to order veggies, refresh lists for groceries and exotic recipes for dishes with names that you couldn't pronounce [like what the hell is a Baba Ghanouj? I'm not putting any Baba in my mouth!] One of my colleagues who I will avoid naming to save him embarrassment, decided to do a final spell-check just before we went into print. And he did a find and replace all on 'tsp' to 'tbsp'. Fortunately, Azhar Shamim [he he!] decided that advertising was not meant for him, though I suspect it was the other way round. And we managed to save the guide and the account.

When designing Branded Content, remember that the person you're targeting is first and foremost an audience. And second, a consumer. *But they are both the same person!* And you have to strike the right balance between Brand & Entertainment. After all, you're trying to build a relationship with your customers. And the best way to do that is by creating content they'll love.

WHY IS BRANDED CONTENT SO DAMN IMPORTANT TODAY?

We live in a world where air, water, food and mobile phones with high-speed internet are absolute essentials. That too, not necessarily in the same order. Mobility is not just the convenience of the latest, fastest, hottest mobile phone with a camera that can photograph the sun, photoshop you with a 6-pack into it and auto-upload it to all your social media handles while generating 4200 likes and 500 new followers... it's a lifestyle! We've got everything we want right at our fingertips. It's all just a tap away.

Leaking tap? Tap... Urban Company. Want to upgrade your breakfast table? Tap... Pepperfry. Hungry? Tap... Zomato, Swiggy. Running low on groceries? Tap... Big Basket, Amazon, Blinkit. Need a ride? Tap... Uber, Ola, Lyft. Craving some tunes? Tap... Spotify, JioSaavn, Apple Music. How about a movie? Tap... BookMyShow. Prefer to stay in? Tap... Netflix, Prime Video. Don't want to do that alone? Well, there's an app for that too. Tap... Tinder, Bumble, TrulyMadly.

You see, we're used to getting exactly what we want, when we want it. It's all about personalized experiences and instant gratification. But here's the thing: we've also become masters at refusing to pay for anything we don't need. Forget cord cutters, there's an entire generation that's a cord virgin! We choose subscription-based platforms over ad supported ones. We use ad blockers like it's nobody's business. We're willing to pay a premium for uninterrupted viewing and seamless experiences. We want to jump the line and get what we want, right now.

You can't buy our time anymore. You can only earn it. That, my friend, is where Branded Content steps in. It's about creating content that's so damn good, so entertaining, that we *willingly* give our precious time to watch it. We're talking about content that doesn't feel like an ad, but like a genuine experience. It's about making a connection, capturing our attention, and earning our loyalty.

In this on-demand world, you've got to crack Branded Content. It's the secret sauce to winning over the hearts and minds of today's audience. These folks are not just consumers, they're the almighty gatekeepers of their own time. And let me tell you, time is precious, mitron. We learned that the hard way during the pandemic and those never-ending lockdowns.

Entertainment rules, ok!

Even in the darkest of times, we always crave entertainment. It's like an essential nutrient for our souls. And you can see it in the unbelievable amount of content being produced and devoured. I mean, just on YouTube alone, 500 hours of videos are uploaded every freakin' minute! And get this, 5 billion videos are watched on YouTube every single day. Global streamers like Netflix, Disney+, Prime Video, Apple TV+, Disney+, HBO Max and Paramount+ spent upwards of US$ 26.5 billion on original content in 2023. It's like all these guys got a shot of super-charged black coffee alongside their vaccines. We're thirsty for more!

Learn from Unbranded Entertainment

So, when Tinder is out there battling Bumble for attention, it's not just competing against other dating apps. No, no no! It's going head-to-head with the likes of Karan Johar and Sanjay Leela Bhansali on one end, and the talented Nora Roberts and Nora Ephron on the other. Thums Up, our desi cola isn't just up against Red Bull. It's fighting for attention with the adrenaline pumping

Rohit Shetty, SS Rajamouli and the Fast & Furious franchise on one side, and the gripping stories of Dan Brown and the new Last of Us game on the other. It's like bringing a knife to a gun fight!

That's where Branded Content comes to the rescue. You've got to load up your arsenal. Instead of competing, it's time to collaborate. Take a page from the book of Unbranded Content and learn their tricks. And *then*, it's time to fight. Bring the heat with your branded messages and leave a mark that can't be ignored.

In this wild, ever-evolving landscape, Branded Content still has a fighting chance. So, gear up, gather your creative troops. It's time to blend the best of both worlds and unleash a wave of captivating content. That's when the audience will eat it up like a bag of movie theatre popcorn. Let the battle begin... Tap!

The Story of 200 insignificant objects

A journalist named Rob Walker and an author named Josh Glenn embarked on a wild social experiment back in 2009. They scoured thrift stores, garage sales, and all the bargain bins you can imagine, scooping up objects that cost no more than a few measly dollars. We're talking hairclips, cane baskets, key rings, bottle-openers – you name it!

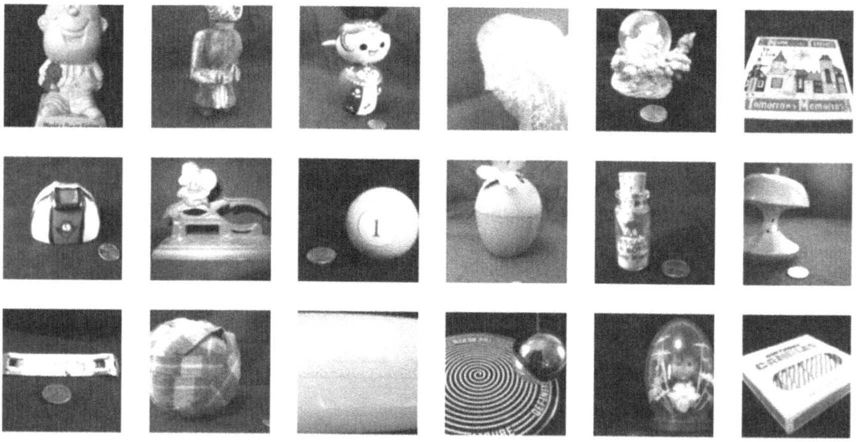

200 'insignificant' objects that became significant through storytelling! Check out: significantobjects.com

But here's where the magic happened. They paired each object with a writer, who was tasked with conjuring up a fictional story about that little trinket. Suddenly, an utterly useless thingy transformed into a "significant" object of desire. These newly minted significant objects were then listed on the auction block of eBay, ready to be claimed by the highest bidder. The winning bidders received not only the object itself but also a printout of its magnificent fictional tale.

And wait for it – these seemingly insignificant doodads that were snatched up for an average price of US$ 1.25 each ended up raking in a whooping US$ 8,000 totally! Ka-ching! The proceeds went to the clever authors and non-profit creative writing organizations. It's like the ultimate win-win situation.

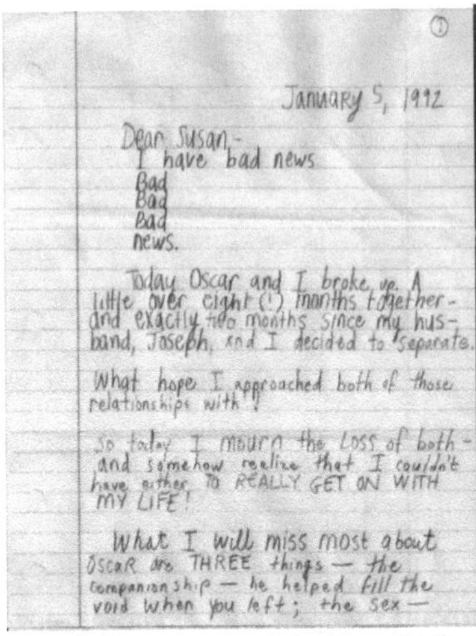

①

January 5, 1992

Dear Susan-
I have bad news
Bad
Bad
Bad
news.

Today Oscar and I broke up. A little over eight (!) months together - and exactly two months since my husband, Joseph, and I decided to separate.

What hope I approached both of those relationships with!

So today I mourn the loss of both - and somehow realize that I couldn't have either to REALLY GET ON WITH MY LIFE!

What I will miss most about Oscar are THREE things — the companionship — he helped fill the void when you left; the sex —

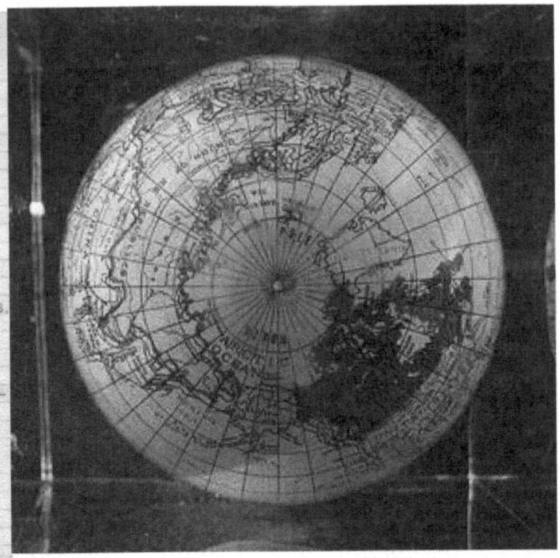

Globe paperweight bought for US$ 1.49, sold eventually for US$ 197.50

Let's take a moment to appreciate the power of storytelling, shall we? Take, for instance, this unassuming globe paperweight. Believe it or not, it came with its very own reality show. Yeah, you heard me right. A handwritten letter to a friend sparked by a saga of broken marriage, torrid affairs, world travels, regret, and the unbearable weight of loneliness. It became a heart-wrenching reminder of multiple romantic failures. This seemingly insignificant object clearly was highly significant to someone. And to someone else who connected with its story. Originally purchased for a laughable US$ 1.49, it eventually sold for a mind-boggling US$ 197.50. People's buying decisions are like a wild rollercoaster ride of rationality and emotion. Quality, service, and value matter, sure, but what they really LIKE can override ALL rational thinking. It's like falling head over heels in love with someone who's clearly an idiot. But hey, love makes us do strange things!

Stories and entertainment have this incredible ability to tap into our emotions, build trust, forge connections, and deliver immense value to both the consumer and, let's not forget, ourselves. Now that's a significant lesson, no?

The Science of Storytelling

There's an epic scene in one of my favorite films, 'Love Actually' by Richard Curtis. Liam Neeson's on a park bench next to his son, Sam. They're having a serious heart-to-heart because little Sammy has been down in the dumps lately. Liam's worried it might be some bully at school or worse. [Can you imagine Liam going all 'Taken' on a kid? *"I will find you and I will kill you!"* Whoops, wrong movie!] Anyway, turns out the boy is in love, and Liam is both, relieved and amused. To which Sam replies, *"What could be worse than the total agony of being in love?"*

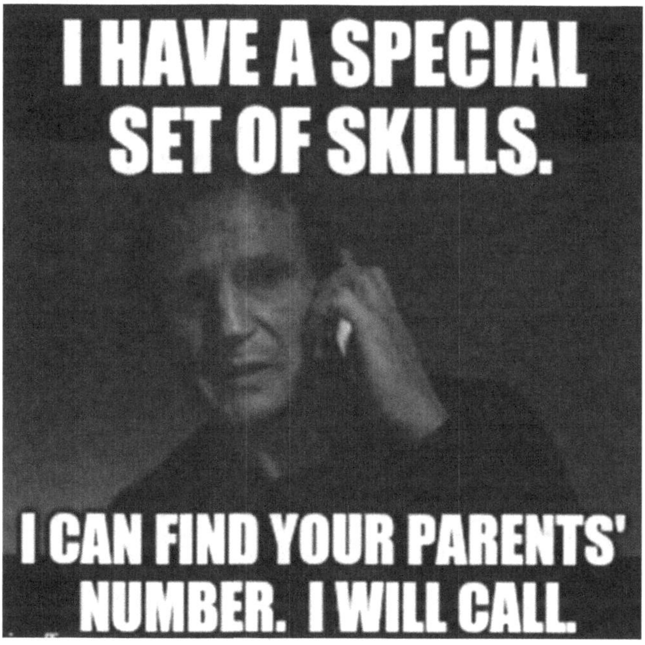

Liam Neeson, NOT in Taken

And it's true, isn't it? Why are love, storytelling, and entertainment so damn powerful? Why do they have this inexplicable hold on us? It's because storytelling is the ultimate brain trickery. It's the art of stirring up emotions that simple descriptions could never evoke. It's like a magical potion for your mind, and boy, does it have an impact on your heart – and your wallet too, sometimes!

Now, indulge me as I go into a little bit of scientific mumbo-jumbo. You see, entertainment and stories delivered by skilled storytellers have the power to mess with your hormones as much as that prescription from your doctor.

There are two sets of hormones at play here: the Pop-Rock Playlist and the Headbangers Ball.

Tom Cruise serving up Cocktails and Dreams

The Pop-Rock Playlist

Drops tracks and beats that trigger the happy, feel-good hormones like...

Dopamine

- It's the hormone that helps you focus, enhances your memory, and even motivates you
- And you know what triggers it? Suspense and cliff-hangers
- That's why those season finales and mind-bending twists leave you craving for more like a love-struck puppy
- Coca-Cola's 'The Happiness Machine' was a series of videos showcasing a special vending machine placed in various locations. It surprised people with unexpected acts of kindness and joy – when they approached the machine to purchase a coke. From Coke, flowers to even pizzas. The videos teased what's next and hinted at a new location where the machine would appear, leaving you eager for more

Coca-Cola's 'The Happiness Machine' campaign

Oxytocin

- It's about building trust, bonding and even driving generosity
- This hormone comes into play when you build empathy, when you make people feel all warm and fuzzy inside
- It's the secret sauce behind those pro-social, CSR campaigns that aim to tug at your heartstrings
- The Dove 'Real Beauty Sketches' is a great example of this. The videos featured an artist who sketched women based on their self-descriptions without seeing their faces. Then the same women as described by strangers they'd met briefly. When compared side by side it revealed that women's self-perceptions were often more critical and less accurate than how others saw them. The videos resonated deeply with the viewers, it challenged beauty norms and promoted a more inclusive definition of beauty that encompassed all shapes, sizes, ages and backgrounds

Dove Real Beauty Sketches

Endorphin

- The feel-good hormones, they make you feel more relaxed, more focused, even more creative
- How do we trigger them? By making you comfortable and making you laugh
- Humor, comedy, slice of life dramas are all tools used to deliver that sweet dose of endorphins straight to your system
- Old Spice's 'The Man Your Man Could Smell Like' is an example that features a really funny character who confidently promotes body wash while delivering rapid-fire comedic lines in absurd scenarios. It made consumers laugh, went viral and became a cultural sensation earning millions and millions of views besides extensive social media buzz

Old Spice, 'The Man Your Man Could Smell Like'

The Headbangers Ball

Bring in the death metal, gangster vibes… and even if you don't want to bite off a bat's head, or smash a guitar against a speaker stack, it still gets your heart jumping and pumping.

Cortisol

- It's the hormone that grabs your attention… but watch it, too much of it can be a buzzkill
- It's triggered by high-stakes drama, the kind that keeps you on the edge of your seat
- Think thrillers that make your heart race faster than Usain Bolt
- Red Bull's genre defying 'Stratos' Space Jump which had Felix Baumgartner jump from the stratosphere, over 24 miles above the Earth's surface is one outrageous example of content that pushes boundaries and solidifies a brand's association with excitement

Red Bull 'Stratos' space jump

Adrenaline

- The hormone that amps up your alertness and excitement levels
- It's like that jolt of energy you get when you're caught up in tension and suspense... induced by stress
- Extreme sports, action thrillers, unexpected plot twists, jump scares – they all know how to inject that adrenaline rush straight into your veins
- BMW's 'The Hire' Series in 2001 were the first of their kind, Hollywood Blockbuster scale production values short films featuring Clive Owen and directed by some of the hottest filmmakers like Guy Ritchie, John Woo, Alejandro Gonzalez Iñárritu among others. Each film featured an action-packed storyline that revolved around a mysterious driver and showcased intense car chases, thrilling stunts and suspenseful narratives. The series became a viral sensation and a benchmark not just in the automobile industry but across categories for Branded Content

BMW 'The Hire' series

But again, too much of headbanging can be a total turn-off. It's like drinking one too many shots at the bar – It can turn you into an irritable, forgetful mess, making questionable life-choices along the way. Kinda like those anti-tobacco PSAs they show in cinemas. Seriously, have you ever met someone who quit smoking because of a guy named Mukesh talking about his phephdas [lungs] and his Maa ka mangalsutra? Yeah, I didn't think so.

But hey, guess what? You're the DJ in this joint. It's up to you to decide what kind of mix you want to serve. The choice here determines the tone, style and content of your Branded Content. Which in turn will determine whether your audience is shaken, stirred or just nursing a bad hangover the next morning.

So, choose wisely, mix your storytelling ingredients with care, blend in the right number of emotions, and serve up a masterpiece that leaves your audience begging for another round. Because in this game, it's not just about the music or the drinks – it's about the experience, the ride, and the lasting impact you leave behind. Cheers to that!

BRANDED CONTENT: THE PERCEPTION VS. REALITY [HA HA!]

Reality check time. A lot of marketers and creators have this wild misconception that Branded Content is a piece of cake. That once they jump on to that brand wagon, they'll instantly unlock the secret formula for marketing success.

They believe, they'll tell an amazing branded story, and suddenly everyone will lose their minds, tripping over themselves to buy their stuff. And voila! Paison ka nangaa naach [you'll be rolling naked in bundles of cash].

Branded Content Process: The Perception

Tell a branded story	➡	It's a superhit	➡	Everyone buys my stuff	➡	Nangaa naach

Spoiler alert: NO.

That's NOT how it goes down. It's more like a never-ending marathon. Not a sprint. Down a long, winding road. With potholes. And detours. And diversions. And untamed creatures. And credit card salespersons. Oh, and did I mention there's no water and sometimes no lights? [But that's why you've got this book, right? Ha ha!]

Here's the harsh reality…

Step one: Tell a great branded story. Two things can happen. Your audience may or may not even see it. Yeah, they could stroll or scroll right past like its wearing Harry Potter's invisibility cloak.

If they see it, that's great. But if they don't... Start again. Find a way to get it in front of their eyeballs. And to do that, you may need to sort how to reach them or try a new or different story altogether.

Step two: If they do see it. Two things can happen. Your audience may like it/ find it relevant or they might not give a flying potato about it. If they do like it, great job! If they do love it, even better. But if they don't... yup, you got it. Start from scratch. Try a different story altogether.

Step three: If they do like it. Two things can happen. They might want more/ be open to seeing/ hearing more. If they love it, they will surely want more. So, guess what? Start all over again. But you will need to find a fresh, different story, build on this one or try a different take that'll keep 'em hooked. This audience tends to get bored faster than a toddler.

And you know what? You'll need to do this over and over. And over and over again. It's like a never-ending merry-go-round. But if you stick with it and keep delivering, eventually you'll build a bond with the audience.

And when the time comes, when they need a product or service that you also offer, that bond will be the reason they choose you. Out of the gazillion other options out there, they'll pick you. They'll buy your stuff.

And if their experience is good, the cycle will repeat over and over. And over and over again. And over time, you may just find yourself doing the paison ka nangaa naach [Well, okay, keep your underpants on for decency's sake].

Branded Content Process: The Reality

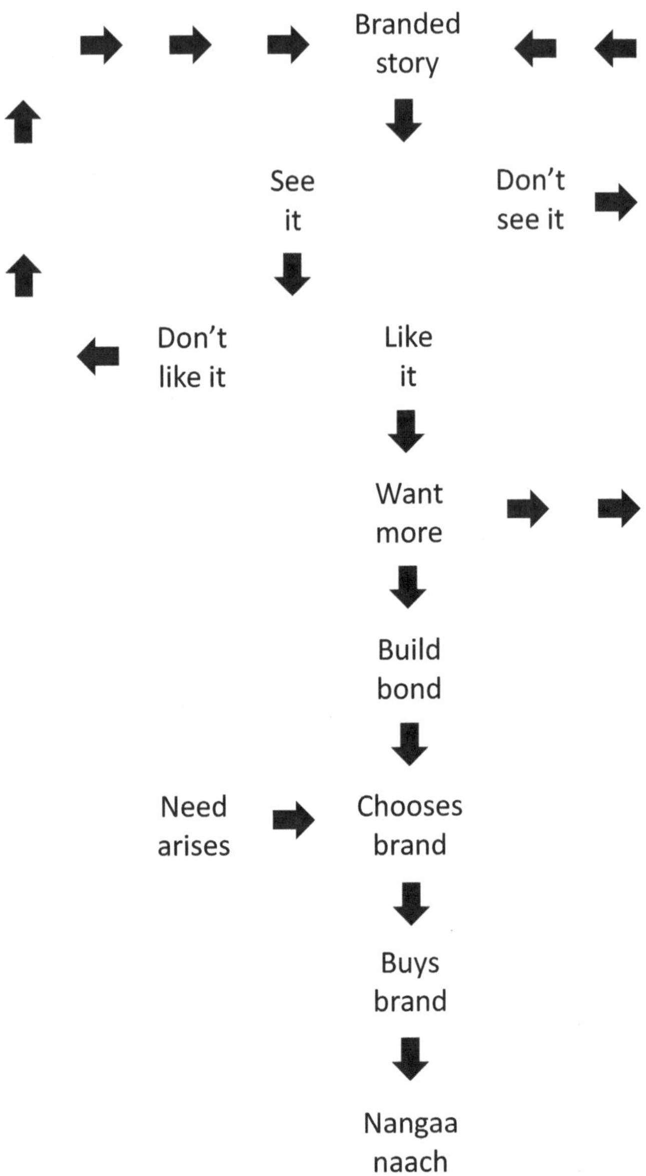

So, that's the reality of the Branded Content process. It might sound like a torturous journey that makes you want to tear this book to shreds and use it as toilet paper. Well, don't do anything rash. The pages here are made of sandpaper and may give you a bad rash. And as looooong and painful as it seems, it actually works. I've seen it in action across categories and genres. So, hang in and start practising your nangaa naach!

Of course, in every system, that includes you, yourself, there will be cynics. The ones who want to play 'devil's advocate' in meetings. The ones you want to stab with ballpoint pens. These are the guys who will still have a ton of arguments against doing Branded Content or anything non-traditional. So, let's try and counter those in advance on the brand/ marketing side first...

"Branded Content is such a waste of money; we'd rather use our budgets for performance related marketing."

Wrong. When your advertising is just bypassed, that is a bigger waste. Cutting media/ brand investment in pursuit of pure performance is "very short-term" and "not sustainable over the long-term". Quotes Mindshare's Global CEO, Adam Gerhart, *"We've got big brands and businesses that are starting to actually see it take an impact and some ramifications on brand equity."*

"Branded Content is ok for established, big brands, we are too new, too small to do this now."

Wrong. In fact, for a start-up brand, branded content is a great, smart, surrogate of earning consumer interest and time. Zomato,

Ching's were all young, challenger brands that leveraged that power to create serious business impact. Irrespective of what stage of the product cycle you are in, this is an important tool in your kitty.

"How do you even know if Branded Content works? It's all touchy feely stuff that can't be measured."

Wrong. You can even measure how much someone loves you! And you can only make stuff better if you can measure it. If you have clear line of sight on your business/ marketing objectives, you will be able to measure the tools that you deploy to achieve them. For branded content at a broad level, it will be whether you were able to bring in the right audiences/ if you were able to keep them engaged/ and finally if you were able to move them to a next step. There's a more detailed chapter on measuring the effectiveness of Branded Content later in this book.

"How do you know when we are doing too much Branded Content?"

Well, on entertainment content, there's no such thing as too much of a good thing. Because if not yours, the consumer may be consuming someone else's content. Then you'd rather have that content be yours' instead. Of course, you can work with the media/ distribution/ planning team to ensure that you optimise it's reach and that each asset is able to reach as many people as possible. This could be through repurposing it across different formats, languages, versions, flipping a video into an audio podcast, a text blogpost, a photo album, a slide show and more.

"Are you suggesting Branded Content replace traditional advertising?"

Wrong. Branded Content is meant to supplement your traditional advertising. It won't work in isolation. Take Red Bull, which has a full-fledged media company, TV channel and more. They still continue to do their short 'Red Bull gives you wings' animated spots. It will help your advertising work harder. And it needs to be part of the overall marketing plan.

"But we don't know how to do this, nor do our current agencies/ partners. Let's stick to the safe, tried and tested."

Now, that sounds like a death-mission, no? Just because you don't know how to do something right now, doesn't mean you don't try it. There are parts of all business processes from manufacturing, sales, after-sales to promotions that get outsourced to the relevant experts. You work with the right team; skill up and then integrate. *But to stick to the safe will be the riskiest thing you can do today!*

"Does Branded Content even work?"

Yes. You can find and quote case studies from practically every product/ service category – several of them featured in this book, both global and Indian examples – to build your case. It's a long tail, but I've seen it work across categories. Consistently.

"Can't AI do this?"

No. Not for now anyway. This is a larger conversation or debate. Automation will take away a lot of mundane tasks. But the big ideas will always come from human intervention. From that one twisted mind that will use AI and tech to analyse the data, the insights, to turn and churn them and then come up with an idea that hopefully blows you and the audience away. You can use tech/ AI again to produce/ execute the idea, to distribute it, to customize it – like a lot of brands have done so well – be it Mondelez's Shahrukh Khan Diwali custom ad, their custom Birthday Song, the Say It with Oreo with Farhan Akhtar or Netflix's UGC driven campaign for the latest season of Black Mirror. As Ted Sarandos, CEO, Netflix said, "Use data to pick stocks, but gut to choose your spouse." And Branded Content is your spouse!

On the creator side, the cynicism will be driven more by a bit of an imposter syndrome and possibly other business concerns, let's try and counter those as well...

"I'm a very new creator with hardly any followers, why will any brand back me?"

No. You can't wait to hit the multi-zillion follower mark to get started. If you have an authentic voice, unique content that serves a highly engaged and clearly targeted audience group, you would be of interest to some brand. I mean even 'nano-influencers' as they call them, are relevant. For Ching's, we landed up targeting even individual, small-time home chefs to promote their Schezwan Chutney.

"But putting a brand message in to my content may dilute it, piss off my followers, audience."

No. You can find a way to strike a balance between brand messaging and entertainment. And if done right, it will add credibility and reach to you, besides revenue.

"What if the brand is a bully and pushes me to create content that is overtly brand skewed?"

Well, you're the expert on the content side, the sensible ones will be happy to work with you, listen to you. Of course, go with solutions rather than a general pushback for all their suggestions. They're also doing their job, and are the ones spending the money. So, give them the confidence that you've got them covered. Try and share a plan on how you plan to integrate the brand, the messaging and the comfort of understanding how you will help them achieve their objectives.

"I don't have any contacts, don't know any brands, agencies, how do I go about approaching them?"

There are several ways to start, including getting representation through an agency. Or cold calls to brands, agencies, writing in with a proposal. There's a chapter on how to build out a proposal, the watch-outs on how to work with brands. But, don't worry, if you're good, you will start to get noticed. Your content will start to get noticed. And then you should hopefully have people reach out to you instead of vice versa. Start already, will ya!

BRANDED CONTENT: TYPES & FORMATS [SO MANY CHOICES, SO LITTLE TIME!]

Everything that's branded is not always entertaining. Just as everything that's entertaining is also not always branded. We've come a long way from the time traditional advertising was restricted by formats. It's time to break free from the shackles of 30 second TV commercials, half-page press ads, and 3:4 hoarding layouts. With digital distribution, the tyranny of durations and multiples of 5 seconds are also gone. We've got tweets, carousels, augmented reality, virtual reality, gaming universes, and so much more at our fingertips. It's like a playground of possibilities, and we're the mischievous kid ready to wreak havoc.

But let me tell you, the duration of a video doesn't determine if it's 'Branded Content'. This is a misnomer with some clients, agencies... where they still believe that a 3 minute 23 second video [but with a logo slapped on the top right-hand corner and a verbal mention in the first five seconds] makes this 'content'. Nope! It's all about the magic that happens within those earned moments that will help you capture hearts, minds and a few wallets along the way.

Branded Content can be delivered in as many formats, genres, types as any content can. Have audience, will entertain! The possibilities are endless.

Some of the different Branded Content formats

Medium	Format
Audio	Song
	Talk show
	Debate
	Talk/ speech
	Poetry, spoken-word

	Stand-up comedy
	Story, fiction/ non-fiction
	Countdown show/ listicle
	Voice-mail, hold music
Video	Music video
	Reality show
	Social experiment
	Documentary
	Fiction series
	Anthology
	Short film
	Feature film
	Tutorial
	Unboxing
	Test/ trial video
	Short form video, reel
	Quiz
	Animation [2D, 3D, stop-motion, flipbook, etc.]
	Talent hunt
	Listicle
	Music, dance performances
	Game-show
Print/ Outdoor	Magazine
	Book
	Newsletter
	Comic, graphic novel
	Cartoon strip, panel
	Blog
	Guide, manual
	Stationery
	Merchandise and even uniforms
	Calendar

	Photo album, gallery
	Hoarding, Out of Home
	Board game
	Presentation, case study
	Product packaging
	Annual report/ financials, sustainability, inclusion, CSR reports
Live/ Event	Conference
	Awards show
	Fashion show
	Workshop, training
	Sports competition, match
	Exhibition
	Concert
Place	Amusement-park, themed ride
	Café, restaurant
	Experience zone/ gallery
	Installation
Digital	Game
	Virtual hangout
	Logo/ Idents [remember the cool animation with MTV logos and the customization for every special day?]
	Webinar
	Social media content
	AR/ VR/ XR
	Out of office auto-replies/ Email signatures
	Wallpapers
Platform/ channel	Branded channel, destination, streaming platform

Now, this is a list of formats, not genres. Think of it like a menu card for entertainment. Within a fiction-series or book you can go from action-packed adventures to thrilling suspense, from hilarious comedies to heart-warming romances, from spine-chilling horror to blood-soaked slashers, and everything in between including detective, drama, sci-fi, fantasy, history, mythology, biopic, sports, mash-ups of these, and so much more. It's like a cinematic buffet where you can mix and match flavors to create your own unique dish.

But wait, these formats aren't confined to a single medium. Oh no, these guys like to play around and dabble in different arenas. For example, everything listed under audio can also be shot, and have a video version. The same applies to all those event-led formats. All of them can also be deployed on digital... but digital here lists things that are natively designed as digital.

Now, I must warn you, this list is by no means exhaustive. There are new formats being discovered and invented as we speak. A good exercise would be to find examples of these formats and see how brands have brought them to life. It's like a scavenger hunt for entertainment, and the prize is a big ol' dose of inspiration.

Factors to Determine What Format of Branded Content is Right for You

Choosing what format or type of Branded Content to use is a bit of a thrilling adventure in itself. Much like choosing the perfect outfit for a red-carpet event. It requires careful consideration of various factors to ensure you make a splash that leaves a lasting impression. Here are a few things to consider:

1. **Know Thy Brand:** First things first, you need to understand your brand's personality, values and target audience. Is your brand bold and edgy like a superhero in spandex? Or perhaps it's more elegant and refined like a sophisticated spy in a tailored suit. Understanding your brand's essence will help guide you toward the format that best aligns with its character. E.g.: If it's a quirky brand like ITC's Bingo chips, the content typically can't be a soppy romantic story. If it's a high-energy brand like Red Bull then you can't be doing a slow slice of life. Of course, don't be afraid to break the rules and surprise them often enough!

2. **Audience Appeal:** Next, you want to think about your audience. Are they tech-savvy millennials who spend their days glued to the screens? Or maybe they're adventure-seeking adrenaline junkies looking for their next thrill? Understanding who your audience is and how they consume content will help you choose a format that grabs their attention and keeps them hooked.

3. **Storytelling Power:** Different formats offer different storytelling opportunities. A song can capture emotions in a few minutes, while a feature film can take audiences on an epic journey. A web series allows for ongoing engagement, and a short film can deliver a powerful message in a compact package. Consider the story you want to tell and choose a format that amplifies its impact.

4. **Budget and Resources:** Let's talk dollars and cents, shall we? The available budget and resources will play a significant role in determining the format you can realistically execute. Feature films can be big-budget productions, while a short film may offer more cost-effective options. Assess resources and align them with your creative ambitions.

5. **Brand Integration Opportunities:** Branded Content thrives on seamless brand integration. Consider which format offers ample opportunities to organically incorporate your brand into the narrative. Can your brand be a character in a web series? Or perhaps it can provide the backdrop for a song or feature film? Find the format that allows your brand to shine without feeling forced.

6. **Flexibility and Adaptability:** Flexibility is key in the ever-evolving world of Branded Content. Consider formats that offer adaptability to different platforms and allow for content extensions. A web series can be repurposed into bite-sized episodes for social media, reels and more. While a feature film can spawn spin-offs or merchandise. Think long-term and choose a format that provides room to grow.

There's no one-size-fits-all answer. The right format for Branded Content depends on a delightful cocktail of factors unique to each brand and campaign. So, go, be bold and choose the format that will best unleash your brand's magic.

Examples of Different Branded Content Formats

1. **Song/ Music Video:** We all remember those jingles that got stuck in our heads like chewing gum on a hot summer day. I mean who can forget the classic washing powder Nirma commercial with Rekha, Hema, Jaya, Sushma... they were practically part of our extended family! But we're not talking about mindless repetitions of the brand name in a song here.

That worked in the past, but won't anymore, given the sheer clutter. We're talking about songs that capture the brand's essence, vibes, and have you jamming on repeat.

Dumb Ways to Die

Melbourne Metro created a catchy song/ video with cartoon characters meeting hilarious ends. It not only became a massive hit, picking up a ton of awards and media but also reduced railway accidents by a whopping 21%. Talk about saving lives through catchy tunes!

Melbourne Metro's 'Dumb Ways to Die' campaign

Fevicol Se from Dabangg 2

Dabangg was already a massive franchise with Bollywood superstar Salman Khan. The original had organically placed a balm/ pain-killer ointment brand, 'Munni Badnaam Hui/ Zandu Balm Hui'. This time round, the producers knew they had to monetize the opportunity. And they took brand integration to a whole new level with Indian glue brand Fevicol. Plugged into the main hook line of the chorus, with a sizzling dance number featuring Salman and Kareena Kapoor, it exploded on airwaves, music channels, and even at awards shows. Stickiness never sounded so good!

Fevicol Se from Dabangg 2

2. **Reality Series:** Now, reality shows are a dime a dozen, but I'm not talking about your run-of-the-mill sponsored segments and shameless plugs. I'm talking about shows that were designed with brands in mind, creating a seamless fit that had audiences hooked.

MTV Hero Honda Roadies

One of the earliest reality shows done in India was designed especially for a two-wheeler brand, Hero Honda [now Hero Motors] for their new launch, the Karizma. The show designed by MTV India in 2003 created a road trip adventure like no other. Young contestants competing, facing challenges, and riding their way to be crowned the ultimate Roadie. It became a cult sensation with its fresh format and organic integration.

Being part of the original launch teams, I got a chance to really help shape it over the first 6 seasons when I was heading MTV India. In those days, it was massive.

MTV Hero Honda Roadies 5, when the show went international

3. **Music Property:** From simple studio sessions to becoming a genre of its own, music properties like Coke Studio have become legendary, setting the benchmark for folk/ fusion and

are go-to references for producers to even describe a sound, *"Coke Studio type ka gaana chahiye!"*

Coke Studio

Coke Studio Pakistan that sets the gold standard is part of pop culture, defining a sound that resonates across geographies. There have been several poor knock-offs tried by everyone from Coffee to Car brands but the original rules.

Coke Studio Pakistan with the chartbuster 'Pasoori'

4. **Feature Film:** From Volkswagen in 'The Love Bug', 'Herbie Goes Bananas' to Rajdoot bikes in Subhash Ghai's 'Hero'. Brands have made appearances in movies. Some with massive impact organically, like the Ray-Ban Aviators in Top Gun. But there's one brand that nailed it like no other.

The Lego Movie

In 2014, Lego took the world by storm with a genre-defying film that mixed animation, live-action, and stop-motion. The brand, its products, the blocks, the characters and the conflict of different types of consumers were absolutely core to the narrative. It picked up a ton of awards, and nominations beyond marketing/ advertising including an Academy Award nomination for best song, clocking close to US$ 70 million at the box-office. Who knew building blocks could build an epic cinematic adventure like this?

The Lego movie

A more recent example of this is the Barbie movie that's gone on to clock upwards of US$ 1.4 Billion at the box-office for Mattel. The team at the toy company and Warner Bros. also executed over 100 brand partnerships in/ around the movie. Making it an 'event film', so even when it was following a massive franchise like Tom Cruise's Mission Impossible 7 and clashing head on with Nolan's Oppenheimer, it not only held its own, but outperformed both those films!

Margot Robbie & Ryan Gosling as Barbie & Ken painting the box-office pink!

Closer to home, there's **Mere Dad ki Maruti**, that I'd produced and, in fact, came out in early 2013, a year before even the Lego Movie. We'll deep dive on that one in a little more detail later in this book.

5. **Calendar:** Ah, the good ol' days of year-end calendars and diaries. While digital calendars have taken over, there was a time when these physical goodies were highly sought after.

Kingfisher Swimsuit Calendar

When it comes to associating beer with good times, Kingfisher nailed it with their iconic calendar. Bollywood superstars like Katrina Kaif, Deepika Padukone were also first spotted here. With spin-off reality shows, merch, and capturing the essence of cool, it became the must-have for beer enthusiasts and calendar collectors alike.

Deepika Padukone first spotted in the KF calendar

6. **Guide:** There are annual reports that brands publish to make themselves feel important, and there are reports published annually that are like the nerds of the marketing world. But hey, some of these actually serve a purpose. Like the Times Good

Food Guide or those fancy TripAdvisor Ratings that establishments are so proud to display.

Michelin Guide

Believe it or not, this thing was created by a French tyre company back in the 1900s to help drivers find restaurants and mechanics. Talk about branching out! They started rating these places with stars, and now, the addition or deletion of a Michelin Star can make or break a restaurant. It's like the culinary Hunger Games, but with fancy food instead of arrows.

Michelin Guide published annually, the benchmark of cuisine and quality

7. **Quiz:** Remember those quizzes we used to do in school? Good times, eh? Well, turns out quizzes aren't just for nerdy teachers anymore. Trivia buffs everywhere are getting their fix in sports,

movies, and current affairs. They're even playing quiz games on apps like Kahoot during game nights with friends and family.

Bournvita Quiz Contest

One quiz show that has stood the test of time is the Bournvita Quiz Contest. Started in 1972 as a radio show with Hamid Sayani [jee haan behnon aur bhaiyyo, Ameen Sayani's lesser-known sibling], transitioning into a TV show with quizmaster Derek O'Brien. A clever way for Bournvita to infiltrate schools and associate themselves with smarts and nutrition. Who knew a chocolate drink could be so brainy?

Bounvita Quiz Contest, originally started in 1972 as a radio show sponsored by Cadbury, now Mondelez

8. **Fashion Event:** Fashion may not be everyone's cup of tea, but some fashion events are just too fabulous to ignore. These events create a premium image, generate buzz, and engage trade and consumers alike. Forget about all the sponsorships and brand placements at events like the MET Gala, the Cannes red-carpet. We're talking about brands that design their own iconic fashion properties.

Victoria's Secret Fashion Show

It's not just about supermodels strutting their stuff in hot lingerie down a ramp. This event fuses fashion with music and pop culture, creating an experience that everyone, and I mean everyone, watches out for. With incredible music performances, choreography and a visual spectacle that would make your eyes pop, Victoria's Secret became even hotter than their lingerie.

Victoria's Secret's annual fashion show is all things awesome

And let's not forget **Lakme India Fashion Week.** It became a benchmark fashion event with massive media coverage. Everyone and their catwalk-loving grandma wants to associate themselves with fashion, and the property changed hands over the years, from Amazon to Myntra. But somehow no one else has found the same impact as Lakme.

9. **Social Media Content:** One place where memes, GIFs, moment marketing and more is in 4th gear. And a variety of brands, from Mumbai's Traffic Police to Food Delivery and Streamers flex their content game.

Liquid Death kills online troll

Liquid Death is one of the newest and coolest brands to have launched. Sharp positioning [kill plastic], a distinct brand personality and great content & communication has marked all they've done. Hell, even their CTAs are cool… 'Summon Us!' vs. 'Contact Us at'.

Now the 'Celebs Read Mean Tweets' is a very popular talk-show format, but when a random internet troll decided to diss the product through a comment that said, "I'd rather lick sweat off a fat guy's back than drink Liquid Death!", the gang decided to really up their game and turned that into a massively viral content opportunity. They did a taste test with 10 people, invited people to try the same and put out a hilarious video. Epic win! And [Liquid] Death to the troll.

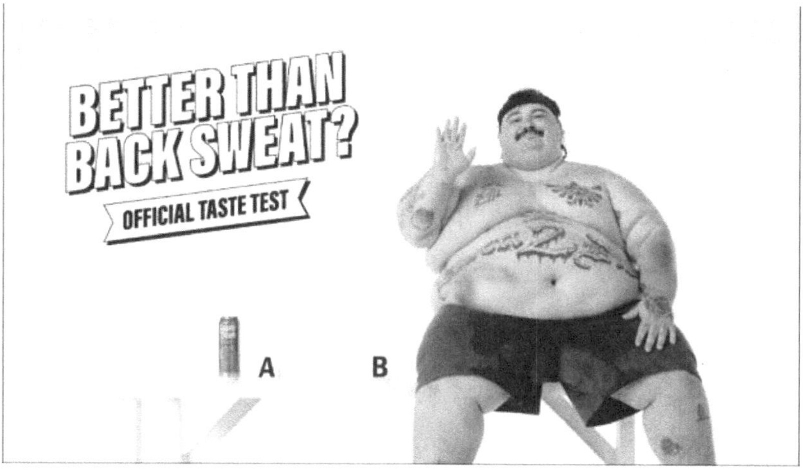

The Liquid Death Taste Test, Do NOT try this at home!

10. **Social experiment:** Several brands have done this, from Dove, Coca-Cola to others. One of my favourites is Carlsberg putting friendship to the test in a genius experiment where someone is asked to call a friend past 2am to see if they will stand up for them, turn up with some cash as they tell them they're stuck and in danger. The friend has to navigate a pretty shady looking space with strange characters, hooligans and more until the reveal and a big gratification for 'Standing up for a friend.'

Carlsberg's social experiment that puts friendship to the test

11. **Place/ Space:** When the actual brand experience can be brought to life through a physical place, space, it can be very powerful. It's like creating a whole new world for consumers to immerse themselves in. It can help cement that bond with consumers besides help generate additional revenue. And when it comes to creating magical experiences, one place reigns supreme.

Disneyland

It's not just about Mickey and friends anymore. With the acquisition of Lucas Films, Marvel, Pixar, and all those other cool franchises, Disneyland has become a goldmine of footfalls and revenue. From ticket sales to merch & meals, they've got it all. It's like stepping into a parallel universe where the movies, shows and characters come alive. And they keep the magic going until the next sequel or spin-off hits. Talk about a never-ending adventure!

Disneyland and their rides are an experience in themselves...

On the installation front, Johnnie Walker did some pretty fun stuff with the Walking Man. But one that really blew my mind recently was the work done for children's charity, The Diana Award. An anti-bullying campaign that came to life with an installation done in a popular shopping mall's atrium. The traditional 'back to school' with new uniforms, school bags and stationery to be bought given a brutal twist with #BackToBullying. Powerful stuff. And really important given that according to statistics, 65% of children are afraid of going back to school because of bullying. It started a very important dialogue on how to make schools safe spaces again.

Search 'Back to School Stunt: The Diana Award'

12. **Platform/ Channel:** Now, here's a big one that requires some serious commitment. Brands stepping into the world of media and content is like a fish riding a bicycle. Yeah, it's not exactly their core area of expertise, but hey, sometimes you gotta shake things up and try something wild.

So, how do brands tackle this daunting challenge? Well, there are a few routes they can take. Some start from scratch and build up the expertise, brick by brick. Others whip out their chequebooks and buy out existing channels. And then there are the savvy ones who team up with established players. Collaboration, my friends, is the name of the game. Most common, and logical.

If it's a large enough piece, it can benefit your core business as well, driving consumers to it besides turning into an independent revenue stream of its own.

Kingfisher did that with NDTV to launch a full-fledged lifestyle channel titled NDTV Goodtimes. Magicbricks.com joined forces with the Times group to create a TV channel dedicated to real estate/ property titled Magicbricks Now. Pepsi did that with MTV for Pepsi MTV Indies. Not all of these stood the test of time. Most faded into the background like yesterday's news. But one that's been amazin' is...

Amazon Prime Video

Started with a simple goal: get people to spend more time on the platform. But this baby grew into a massive offering all on its own. Their shows and films started racking up nominations, picking up awards left and right, and attracting viewers like moths to a flame. Talk about turning a side-gig into a full-blown blockbuster.

13. **Annual Sustainability Report:** Now instead of being a document that all of 4 people read, even something as

'mundane' as a roundup of your sustainability efforts & results can be flipped into some amazing content. Trust the guys at Apple to nail that... with Octavia Spencer and CEO, Tim Cook himself no less.

Mother Nature checks in on Apple

14. **Product Packaging:** A lot of folks have used the real estate on/ in/ around their product packaging to deliver some great messaging. From recipes, to games. Amazon recently did some great 'Storyboxes' in India to motivate their sellers. Stories of entrepreneurs, start-ups were printed on the delivery boxes that went out. And a link/ scan led consumers to a more detailed story and other sellers as well on their site that they could check out. From a homemaker in a small town in Tamil Nadu to indigenous spices from the North East.

Search 'Amazon Storyboxes'

Just like there are countless ways to entertain people, the same, if not more ways exist to integrate a brand or create branded content. You have to choose and use the format that suits your brand's content the best based on your objectives, budgets, ambitions. And here's a little secret: you don't have to choose just one. Mix it up, throw in a variety of formats, and surround your audience with entertainment from all angles. The more, the merrier, my friends.

Potential Opportunities in Branded Content

There are some genres, formats that for some reason have remained untouched by brands which provides a potential opportunity for someone to swoop in and plant a flag on that mountain...

1. **Horror:** Most brands are scared of associating with this genre given the fear/ negative associations. But there's no denying the sheer popularity of Horror. Horror films also have multiple sub-genres from zombie to slasher films, creature to found footage. Now there are 'mash-ups' of horror-comedies and horror-sex! Audiences love a good scare. Some brands attempt tactical campaigns on Halloween. Some life-insurance brands have created communication around death, but no one's really nailed it. And that's a gap waiting to be filled!

2. **Spoof:** Beyond the cliched Sholay take-off and tacky look/ sound-alikes, parodies work well because they juice something that's already loved or hated. At MTV, we were up against the Star TV Network, 120 billboards across the city and Simi Garewal who could pull guests like Laxmi Mittal and Hrithik Roshan. We had a boy in a skirt dressed as her – Cyrus Sahukar as Semi Girebaal – to take on the assault. It was genius counter-scheduling at the same time-slot, Sundays, 9.30pm. And we took them down! Because people loved calling out what looked fake or pretentious! You could no longer look at Simi without thinking of Semi! And it worked so seamlessly with Sprite that was playing with the whole 'No bakwaas, Sprite clear hai' narrative at that stage.

Many successful content creators like TVF with their Qtiyapa series, AIB to others started out with spoofs before they pivoted to originals. Fully Faltoo at MTV was a genre in itself.

Cyrus Sahukar as Semi Girebaal in the MTV spoof

3. **Comics:** We all grew up on graphic novels, comics, digests, illustrated magazines, picture books. And there is still a large enough dedicated audience for it. Amul does a still, single slide version of that through their dedicated billboards. BSA SLR cycles used to have a comic strip featuring Kapil Dev. Myntra recently did a version with a tribute to the school community living 'Adarsh Balak' [ideal child] charts for their 'End of Reason Sale'. It's a format that could find a fit beyond kids. Ask anyone with a Batman or Manga collection!

Kapil Dev on BSA SLR, there's also one with Vijay Amritraj

Myntra's End of Reason Sale with the 'Adarsh Baalak' take-off

4. **Documentaries:** Non-fiction content in India has usually meant terrible talent hunts, shiny stage competitions, reality shows with annoying contestants and crafted drama. But the consumption of compelling docus across Vice and even mainstream OTT platforms now shows what an opportunity this can be. They have the added advantage of coming with in-

built trust. I'm not talking about a factory tour or a biography of the Company's founder, but a theme that has a broader relevance with the audience. Like Cyber-Security in today's times being taken on by a laptop brand, and more. Or a vegan [stop smirking!] food brand taking on a docu on the harmful side-effects of processed food.

5. **Courses:** Beyond DIY, tutorial and recipe videos, edutech has seen an explosion. There's a course for everything, including how to conduct or create an online course. And people are willing to even pay to upskill if you can offer the right value. You can potentially barter their time for the right content, if you can design a masterclass on a subject of relevance to your consumer. Healthier living/ eating for a food brand. Doing up the house dirt cheap by a paints/ furniture brand. Getting stylish on a budget. Beyond the cooking recipes, of course.

6. **Books:** Yeah, there's a reason why the film usually never matches up to the book – no Blockbuster movie even with the biggest star, director, VFX or budget can ever match up to the theatre of the mind. That's why there's such a resurgence in reading. Strangely no brand has been able to capitalize on this – be it creating a character with its own book series or embedding a brand into a popular book series. Publishers, authors, brands... you listening?

7. **eSports:** It's just too big to ignore. Bigger than movies and music put together. The perceptions about only nerds being into gaming, that it's too violent and that it's not a real sport – are just that. Perceptions. There's an entire generation that likes to watch people play online games. There's no reason for

this to feel weird. We spend millions of dollars to watch athletes play other games, don't we? It's the ultimate digital-born sport with digital-born stars and consumers. When I produced a show called Gamer's Den for MX Player [India's largest OTT platform] profiling some of India's hottest new and upcoming gamers, I was surprised to see the mix of people showcased – from a 17-year-old girl from Mira Road to a simple Gujarati boy. Their dedication to the craft, their investment, it was nuts. It's pretty much like the stories we hear about any other sport. And you will be shocked to hear the ticket size of prizes on these competitions.

Even casual mobile gaming is just massive. I got a chance to help on character design for one of those really popular parking games with Games2win – Parking Professor. And the engagement with consumers, is just off the charts. Now the opportunity to embed cars, incentives and more is amazing here.

Games2win's Parking Professor game

8. **Games and New Sports:** Some of the traditional sports, like Cricket, Football, are too cluttered with a zillion brands fighting for attention. Even Kabaddi, Badminton, Hockey, Wrestling are starting to pick up momentum with their own leagues. The opportunity is to go after some lesser-known sports – be it Table Tennis or creating new sports altogether. Like Red Bull did with the Soap Box race. It's a spectacle with people creating their own versions of vehicles, dressing up and then rolling down a slope!

Sport is where I've seen grown men cry when their teams win or lose. It's where consumers will paint their face blue. It's live, social, and global. It's non-stop unscripted drama. And brands need to think beyond sponsorships. Just having their logos on a jersey will not magically plant you into the audience's heart! They will need to become active participants. Consumers are hugely underserved on this. There are very compelling stories [look at Rinku Singh of KKR or Yashasvi Jaiswal of Rajasthan Royals on the IPL, they're movies waiting to happen!], see what the NBA does with fashion, music, art, entertainment, film. It's a multi-cultural, multi-genre crossover. And you don't need to be a sports brand to do this.

Does Size Matter? Aka Chal Jhoothi!

One big misconception to tackle head-on. The myth that audiences these days have the attention span of a goldfish on a caffeine high. Seriously who came up with that nonsense? Probably someone who couldn't hold a goldfish's attention for more than a second.

So, here's the truth: it's not about the length, it's about the strength. Size doesn't define the power of a piece. Take a moment to let that sink in. The audience we're talking about can binge-watch a 12-hour season of Money-Heist without breaking a sweat. They can game for a mind-boggling 15 hours straight. These folks are no joke.

The real key to capturing their attention lies in the quality of your messaging and content. Yeah, those first five seconds in a branded content piece, the opening line of a novel, or the kickass opening scene of a film – they matter. They're like the appetizer that hooks you in. But let's be honest, this challenge applies to all forms of content – branded or unbranded.

We've all been there, right? Watching a movie and thinking, "Damn this director really needs a better editor." That comic who was fantastic for 1 hour 10 minutes but when stretched to 1 hour 20, you were like, "When is he going to finish?" Or, reading a book that could've wrapped up in 20 pages but stretched to 200? It happens.

Sure, there are platforms where short cat videos and random dance challenges give this audience a quick fix. But to claim that's all they have headspace for? That's a wild over-generalization. They don't give a flying donut whether it takes 15 seconds or 15 hours – as long as it entertains them, they're game.

Don't be afraid of the audience's time, value it. You can't buy it off a shelf anymore, you gotta earn it. By using all the tools, formats, ideas and their cousins at your disposal.

SURROUND CONTENT AROUND BRANDED CONTENT

Let's face it, people these days aren't just channel surfing. They're book surfing while pumping iron at the gym, listening to music as they casually text their latest dating app match. They're master multi-taskers hopping across platforms like kangaroos on steroids.

You gotta be where they are. That's why we looked at so many formats in the last chapter. Your primary content can be on one primary medium, but the idea needs to be platform-agnostic. Now surround them with a whirlwind of ideas and extensions that lead them straight to your primary platform. It's like a stealthy ninja attack, but with content.

Surround, ancillary or shoulder content. Lot of names, but it's the extra spice that makes Branded Content even more delicious. It's like when you order a burger and it comes with a side of fries, onion rings, and a mini parade of condiments. Surround content is the extra oomph that keeps your audience hooked and craving for more.

In the movie biz, they've been doing it forever. From posters, teasers, trailer to songs, scenes, interviews, and even hilarious bloopers – there's a whole buffet of content to feast on.

And it has a ton of advantages...

Surround Content can Extend the Shelf-life of your Branded Content

Today the shelf-life of things has really shrunk. Hell, people change their display pictures and WhatsApp status more frequently than they change their underwear. [Well, some just turn 'em over inside out, but I digress.] Songs don't stay on the charts for weeks, and movies don't celebrate silver jubilees [25 weeks nonstop in cinemas] anymore. It's a fast-paced world out there. But surround content can engage people in a variety of different ways thereby stretching the lifespan of Branded Content.

Surround Content can Aid the Discovery of your Branded Content

Your audience may or may not always be on the primary platform where you're publishing your Branded Content. But the surround around the content is what they can potentially stumble upon... like finding some clues that lead you to the hidden treasure!

Surround Content can help Build a Deeper Bond with your Branded Content and your Brand

Once people fall in love with your content, they want more. They want to know the name of that amazing actor who had the mind-blowing cameo in your film. They'll start stalking them on Instagram and digging deep into their rap sheet. It's not enough to just love a song by Dire Straits; you gotta know that Sting belted out those iconic words *"I want my MTV!"* and he wrote the damn song after overhearing the carpenters [the workers, not the band] moving furniture in his house. And that Sting's real name is Gordon Summers. Hey, because when it comes to Branded Content, Money, is not just for Nothin'! This, deeper connection with your content makes the audience feel cooler than an ice cube in Antarctica, and they'll spend even more time engaging with your masterpiece. It's a win-win!

Surround Content gives One More Opportunity to Wave a flag at the Consumer at a Smaller Incremental Cost

Since it's an extension, created from existing content, it's usually something that can get made without breaking the bank. And for a minor incremental cost, you can churn out a plethora of content pieces. Each one is a golden opportunity to seamlessly integrate your brand. Some of them as a format may actually warrant a spokesperson reading out the brand vision, a shameless product plug, and maybe even sneaking your boss into the mix. Oh, marketing folks calm down. Here, have some tissues.

Surround Content can Drive More Engagement and, at times, even Incremental Revenue

Sometimes, the surround content can be as compelling as the main attraction. Back when I was heading MTV India, the crew on Roadies was a wild bunch. I mean, seriously, those behind-the-scenes shenanigans were off the charts. So, naturally, we decided to peel back the curtain and give the audience a taste of the chaos with a 'Making of Roadies' series. And what started as a short vignette eventually grew into a full-fledged show of its own. Each crew member, from Bumpy, Chhotu to Ricky and, of course, Raghu became characters that the audience recognized, loved and looked forward to. We had as much drama on a reality TV show about a reality TV show as the reality TV show itself!

The 'Making of Roadies' became a sticky sensation, extending the time spent on the channel and setting social media on fire. We even had a whole separate set of sponsor brands jumping on board the 'making' train. Those episodes rated as high as the main show! It's like the wild side dish stealing the thunder from the main course. But hey, who doesn't love a delicious surprise?

Sample Content Surrounding Branded Content

Let's look at one format of Branded Content and see the variety of ancillary content that can be made around it.

The Song/ Music Video

Sr.	Ancillary Content	Details
1.	Teaser poster	Could be an image, screen grab from the music video. A graphic with lyrics. Something that 'teases' the audience, gets them intrigued but doesn't give away too much. You can do multiple versions of these, but be careful that you don't stretch it too much.
2.	Teaser promo	A short edit/ video that just uses the hook line, or the riff' from the song, with a hint of the star/ singer featured.
3.	Poster[s]	The main reveal announcing the name of the song, the singer, launch date. Multiple versions, different ratios can be done.
4.	Motion Poster	The poster in an animated version with some of the music from the main track.
5.	Trailer	A promo playing out a clip of the song, the main hook line, showcasing some of the highlights, making the audience want to check out the main song/ video.
6.	Song [audio]	Just the audio of the song. What would play out on radio stations, audio streaming platforms.
7.	Music video	The main song in all its glory with the

		music video. Most music is consumed visually these days. People discover/ search for music on YouTube and then play it on repeat on Spotify, Apple Music and more.
8.	Lyric video	Lyrics of the song as graphics, this could be a separate, standalone asset.
9.	Karaoke video	The song minus the vocal track for people to sing along with lyrics appearing like a karaoke video.
10.	Karaoke audio	Audio track minus the vocals for people to make their own covers, engage.
11.	Song dubs	The song can be done in multiple other languages – both local and international. For instance, a Shahrukh Khan film called 'Fan' that we worked on had one title song called 'Jabra Fan'. We created multiple language versions featuring some of the biggest local and international singers to bring in new audiences.
12.	Video [language versions]	You can do a full-fledged new music video in the new language, or slap on the audio to the existing video. For 'Jabra Fan', we featured the singers in the recording studio intercut with footage from the main song. Check out Jabra Fan 11 language mash-up.
13.	Behind the Scenes of the Audio/ Song	A short or long video, featuring the making of the song. From the lyrics, song-writing to the composition, the ideation, the genesis of the song, the brief, the recording with the live musicians, the singer[s] in the studio, the tweaking of the mix, interviews of

		each of the key people involved besides the brand's spokesperson.
14.	Behind the Scenes of the Video	A video that captures the making of the music video, the choreography, set design, construction, lighting, styling, rehearsals, pranks on set, interviews with key crew members, the director, even the spot boy, the briefing process. And the brand spokesperson.
15.	Director's commentary	Video with director's commentary for people to go into what each shot or sequence meant and more.
16.	Song remix	Check out Ed Sheeran performing 'Shape of You' with classroom instruments. Now imagine this being done with a brand's packaging to create music.
17.	Video remix	Each of the remixes can be backed by a simple video with a change in graphics, edit, bringing in new footage, cuts not used in the main edit.
18.	Song unplugged	Acoustic version of the song.
19.	Video unplugged	Check out Diljit Dosanjh performing Ikk Kudi from Udta Punjab.
20.	Stills, photos	Photos from the sets, from the final video, from the behind-the-scenes action, fun moments, cast profiles, crew profiles. This could be candid production stills or a full-on planned photo shoot.
21.	Memes, GIFs	Funny extensions, boomerangs, and more created using clips of the video or parts of lyrics.
22.	Song spoof/ parody	Alternative lyrics, e.g.: 'Papa kehte hain badaa naam karega' becoming 'Papa

		kehte hain badnaam karega!' Before someone else on the internet does it, do it yourself. Like you've been possessed by Weird Al Yankovic, Devang Patel. In the tone of those honest trailers. But this should be done depending on the tone, positioning of your brand, messaging. It may not suit all categories, brands and communication.
23.	Spoof video	A funny version of the video with gags, or funny captions. Check out Bank Chor trailer, a feature film I'd produced. And the spoof of the trailer we did. Search 'Imaandar Trailer Bank Chor'.
24.	Gender flip version of audio	If the original song is in a male voice, then flipping that or vice versa. You could also do a kid's version.
25.	Edits, cutdown promos	Can do multiple edits of this using the chorus, hook line, other elements of the song.
26.	Covers with music influencers	Getting popular digital stars to create their version of the song. Check out an amazing version of Jiya Re from Jab Tak Hai Jaan created by Alaa Wardi. Yashraj Mukhate is particularly popular with his unique takes on corny lines. But be careful not to overdo something that's already been done. Like the product placement of him chomping on some food can be replaced by any brand!
27.	Dance influencer covers	Getting some dance influencers, groups to do a dance-off or their own

		choreography. This can also go out as a dance challenge. Remember Quick Style doing a viral Bollywood mash-up at a wedding?
28.	Collaborations on audio	A version where another singer[s] is invited to jam along with a new version that's put out.
29.	Collaborations on video	Same extended with others for a video.
30.	Live performance of the song	This can also be done in different locations creating a new vibe and going after different cohorts. From a College Campus, to a Senior Citizen's Home, one busking at a public place to a funeral home... ok maybe not the funeral home. Check out Scoop Whoop café with a mash-up of friendship songs at a campus.
31.	Flashmob	Performed in a busy intersection, mall, or somewhere, hell, your brand's showroom! Search Sacla Stage Shopera in London Foodhall.
32.	Contest	A set of contests across platforms linked to different giveaways. To win stuff from the music video like a trip to where it was shot/ a car or vehicle featured/ the clothes worn by the singer/ meet and greet with the stars/ chance to get your own version shot by the same director or more.
33.	Contest – filmmakers	You can try getting film school students to compete to make their own version of the video. Be prepared for some horrid entries too!

34.	Tutorial – dance	The original choreographer and the stars or even any other expert demonstrate how to do the hook step.
35.	Tutorial – how to play [for different instruments]	This can be done by the composer and his sessions musicians or by a music teacher. For different string instruments [guitar, ukulele, violin, other], percussion [drums, bongo, tabla, other], wind instruments [flute, saxophone, trumpet] or even some new, unique instruments.
36.	Tutorial – vocals	The singers show us how to sing the song, the highs, lows, bringing in the fun, the emotion.
37.	Lyric sheet with meaning	With the lyricist, deliver this as spoken word poetry, opening up the meaning of the song. And also provide this with meanings in other languages.
38.	User generated content	Inviting consumers to create their own version, send in their videos. A fresh edit can also be made intercutting that footage – both vocals and video. Search 'Starships performed by Mike Tompkins, the Pitch Perfect cast and You'. Pharrell Williams' 'Happy' had a ton of videos across the globe of people dancing to his song from offices to schools.
39.	Launch event	Releasing the song and music video with a special event showcasing the video to media, featuring the crew for interactions and the brand spokesperson on stage.
40.	Concert	A concert themed around the song

		with the main song as the grand finale but also bringing in other hits around the same concept by other opening acts and more.
41.	Slide share/ case study	Targeting the trade/ business/ marketing side, what you did, how you did it, a case study presentation.

Riding the UGC Wave

A small-note on User-Generated Content. Today thanks to technology and the digital age, content creation has been hugely democratized. Anyone with a basic smartphone has all the tools necessary to create content in their pockets. Most digital creators start out like that. It's not something to resist. Because it's not a wave, it's a tsunami. Flow with it. Instead of fighting it, ride it.

If you remember the Indigo airlines fiasco when they stopped a passenger with autism from flying. Similarly, Starbucks actually had to shut down a bunch of their cafés in the US to retrain the staff against their inherent racial biases after a video someone shot with a barista reacting to some African-American customers went viral.

So, design your content to not just embrace, but allow, encourage UGC. Invite consumers in, let them co-own the content. Intel and Toshiba did with a series titled 'The Beauty Inside'. The story of a guy who woke up in a different body every day had consumers write, act out their own versions of the character get integrated into the story. Check out 'Intel and Toshiba's The Beauty Inside case study'.

UGC is a never-ending engine, it's the cheapest way to generate content. Consumer engagement, at their cost!

Now, I'm not saying you have to go all bananas and do every single thing on this list, but doing at least a few of 'em is crucial if you wanna squeeze out all the juicy benefits of Branded Content. See, it's not just about creating killer content; you also want people to talk about it, share it, and sing its praises. And if you really nail it, you might even pull off some mind-blowing magic. Beyond the brand love and business, you may even change opinions, shift perceptions and maybe even [gulp!] influence some policy.

But always, always start with the story. Not with the surround.

DIFFERENT SCALES AND ROLES OF BRANDED CONTENT

Now, we've got ourselves a few flavors of Branded Content, along with some fancy-pants ancillary content. You can scale these bad boys up or down depending on your marketing objectives and budgets. It's like picking the right superhero for the job, but with less spandex or more marketing lingo.

We're gonna classify these babies into three types, which have more names than a Bollywood star's ex-girlfriends. But we'll stick to the most common one – Hero, Hub and Hygiene. Google came up with this gem for YouTube, but it fits like a perfectly tailored suit for Branded Content too. Let's dive in.

Hero

Hero content is the big daddy of them all, the heavyweight champion. These are the blockbusters, the *"I'm Batman!"* in the Justice League or Captain America if you're a Marvel fan. They cost a pretty penny, require meticulous planning, and boast production values that may make your jaw drop. They don't come around too often, maybe once a quarter, twice a year, or just once in a year or two. Hero content grabs attention, sparks conversations, and reels in fresh audiences. They hit an established fan base, to reengage them. They reinforce your leadership, and expertise. High-impact stuff to drive new subscribers.

It's like those TV shows, KBC ['Kaun Banega Crorepati', 'Who wants to be a millionaire' on Star Plus] or KKK ['Khatron ke Khiladi', 'Fear Factor' on Colors TV] designed to lure viewers in at Prime Time. These bad boys scream, *"Hey, look at us, we're the real deal!"*

Amitabh Bachchan in Kaun Banega Crorepati

An FMCG brand example is 'Ranveer Ching Returns' that I'd produced for Ching's Desi Chinese. It introduced a ton of new audiences to the brand with it's outrageous Mad Max meets Bollywood's Rohit Shetty 5-minute short film.

Ching's got Blockbuster Bollywood Director Rohit Shetty to direct a 5-minute short film featuring Ranveer Singh, Tamannah Bhatia

Hub

Hub content is your regular, recurring stuff. This is the content your loyal fans crave. Audiences expect this from you. Hub content is not as hectic as the heroes in terms of production values, but it's top-notch quality that keeps your audience hooked. You gotta produce this stuff on the reg, from bi-weekly to weekly, or to at least a few times a month. It's all about building credibility, authority, and getting those likes, shares and interactions.

Like those daily soaps, 'Kyunki Saas Bhi Kabhi Bahu Thi' for Star Plus and 'Balika Vadhu' for Colors, that kept people glued to their screens after they came in with the big tentpole shows. Hub content says, *"Hey, we're reliable, and we're here to entertain you regularly!"*

Smriti Irani Mishra as the ideal bahu in Ekta Kapoor's iconic K-series soap, 'Kyunki Saas Bhi Kabhi Bahu Thi' on Star Plus

Hygiene

No, it's not about brushing your teeth or taking a shower – although those are pretty important too. Hygiene content is all about serving the folks who are searching for something specific. Like being their virtual genie, granting their wishes for information and help. You gotta churn this stuff out efficiently, in high quantities, and frequently. We're talking daily, bi-weekly. It could be in the form of daily articles, listicles, FAQs, simpler tutorials.

Even simple DIY and unboxing videos can be dressed up, jazzed up to land more than a smile. Ryan Reynolds is one entertainer-marketer who really knows how to land a knock-out punch for brands. Beyond the brands/ companies he's invested in as well. But some of his best work is on his own brands like Wrexham Football Club, Mint Mobile and Aviation Gin. Check out how a simple Father's Day cocktail recipe shot for under a few thousand bucks can turn into a such a fun spot. This one was called 'The Vasectomy'.

Father's Day Cocktail for Aviation Gin 'The Vasectomy'

Even unboxing videos can be made really fun like the folks at Volvo did recently for the new EV. It featured their CEO talking about how small can be beautiful.

Volvo EX30 Unboxing

For Ching's, this was in the form of multiple recipe videos showing people how to use their Schezwan Chutney. Helping newbies discover and start a beautiful relationship. Hygiene content says, *"Hey, we're here for you, and we've got all the answers you need!"*

Chef Harpal Sokhi giving Chinese a Desi twist for Ching's Secret

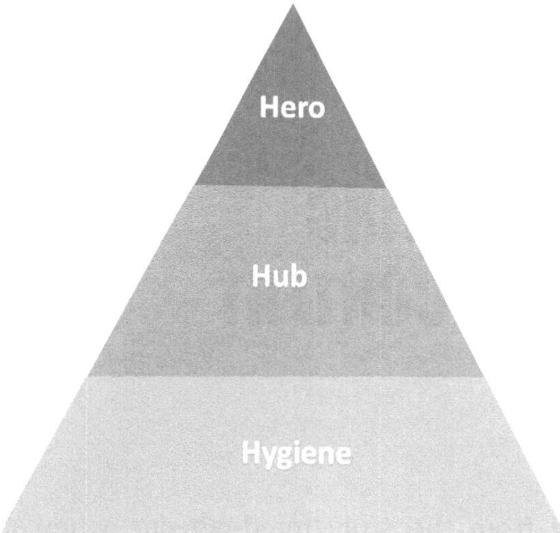

Costs: High
Frequency: Quarterly, Bi-annual, annual
Role: Conversation starter

Costs: Medium
Frequency: Weekly, Fortnightly, Monthly
Role: Conversation keeper

Costs: Low
Frequency: Daily, bi-weekly
Role: Conversation filler

Now, I know some of the hygiene content sounds like your typical ongoing content marketing. But hey, it's an opportunity to turn even the dullest product literature into a page-turner, a chance to entertain and engage the audience at every touchpoint. Heck, I even used to dub the voice-mail greeting/ hold message on the landline/ office reception at the MTV office with a quirky message. Every single interaction with your audience is a shot at turning them into die-hard fans.

It's your chance to become their hero!

EVALUATING BRANDED CONTENT

What separates the good from the truly mind-blowing when it comes to Branded Content? It's like comparing a regular cup of coffee to the one that blows your mind and makes you question the meaning of life. Evaluating Branded Content can be tricky, but we're gonna try and break this down.

There's a two-part checklist: Entertainment. And Branding. It's a delicate dance. You don't want too much entertainment *without* the brand, or people will be like, *"Hey, who are you again?"* And you definitely don't want to drown in branding without the entertainment, or they'll tune out faster than you can say, *"Wait!"*

Elements to Evaluate the Entertainment Quotient

You never know what entertains who, like what's with all those cat videos? But then, there are some fundamental attributes that always help engage an audience. These are the things you look for in any story, branded or not.

1. **Relatability**: Great stories are relatable, familiar. Just like that classic negotiation tactic where you mirror the other person. It sounds corny, but it works. But it's not just about placing characters from your target audience as leads. Stan Lee nailed it with his Marvel superheroes. They have superhuman abilities, but also very human flaws. Take your friendly neighbourhood Spiderman, swinging from skyscrapers, but he has the same relationship issues that hit close to home. Dove's Real Beauty Sketches put 'real women' into the spotlight, making a massive impact.

Spidey worried about the new pimple that's sprouting on his nose

At the heart of a film like Mere Dad ki Maruti was a father and son story. The situation about sneaking out your dad's car, trying to woo the college hottie, were all situations that were hugely relatable. We just pushed them a bit more and, of course, weaved in the Maruti Ertiga beautifully.

2. **Novelty/ Surprise:** Very few film sequels do as well as the original. They're typically liked lesser, seen lesser. As they often get repetitive, with the same characters, the same gags, the same arc. This also happens with brands when messaging gets tired. It's the same story told over and over. Not cool. Your packaging should be recycled, not your ideas! Just replace the stunt in a Mountain Dew commercial, it's the same ad reproduced over and over. Given that now they're up against Fast X at one end and Mission Impossible and Pathaan at the other, it's predictable to the point of being invisible. Audiences want familiarity not predictability.

Bigger stunts, badder villains, higher stakes. Throw in a secret reveal, introduce new relationships and characters, take us on new journeys. Audiences want novelty. They want to be surprised. Remember the 2014 'Devil's Due' horror film with the robotic Devil Baby pranking the streets? Outrageously surprising and viral, generating buzz for the movie.

The Devil Baby prank

In the packaged foods space, specifically noodles, Nestle's Maggi was the category leader since decades. Their hungry kids rescued by a supermom in *"Beta, 2 minutes!"* was a trope that every competitor, from Unilever's Knorr to ITC's Yippee were trying to rip off. The 'cool advertising mommy' was, in fact, generic to most brands/ categories. From noodles to refrigerators.

Ching's Desi Chinese did the unthinkable. It killed the mom. And 'My Name is Ranveer Ching' happened. A fun song & music video that captured the imagination of the trade and consumers alike, driving sampling, and sales. More on this later.

3. **Conflict:** Imagine a story that goes like this: Boy meets girl, they fall in love, get married and live happily ever after. Snooze-fest. Sholay wouldn't be Sholay without Gabbar. Star Wars wouldn't be Star Wars without Vader. A great story bridges what is and what could be, creating tension and keeping us on the edge of our seats.

Think James Bond movies with their epic opening set pieces, or the Black Mirror season pilot where the Prime Minister is asked to do the unthinkable on national TV. Conflict makes stories captivating.

Chipotle did that really well with its award-winning 'Scarecrow' campaign. An animated short film set in a dystopian world that pits the corrupt and mass-produced food industry against sustainable, ethical, and locally sourced food. It used conflict to raise awareness, engage viewers emotionally, and inspire action. And, of course, positioned itself as a brand that stands for a more conscious approach to dining.

Chipotle's 'The Scarecrow' campaign

MTV Roadies with its knock-out format and twists served up in every episode that keep both, the contestants and viewers guessing did that with great impact too.

Now, this creation of conflict and tension is also often a fundamental differentiator vs. traditional advertising. The reason is simple. There is typically little or no time in a 30 second commercial and its 20 second and 10 second cutdowns to build character, set up a conflict. And most agencies, clients are afraid of conflict. They insist on 'cutting to the chase' to hammer in the positive benefits, the features and attributes of the product that enable those. This is true irrespective of the medium. They want the headline in the ad, the hoarding to scream out the product. But every great story relies on tension.

Because without tension there is no attention.

4. **Simplicity:** When I was publishing my Children's Book with HarperCollins, [Goldiboy and the Three Apes], I learnt something really interesting: most people like to recreationally read at 2 levels lower than their typical reading levels. That's why most blockbuster novels are at the 6th grade level. JK Rowling, Ernest Hemingway, Stephen King. Great stories speed you along. You don't think about the words.

Filmmakers like Raju Hirani, James Cameron get this completely. It's not just about appealing to the lowest common denominator or dumbing things down. They tackle complex concepts but make them digestible. Be it aliens or Gandhi's philosophy. So, when you're creating branded content, keep it fluent. Don't call in Shashi Tharoor to write your script. Unless a dictionary comes with your product for free.

Take Seagram's Imperial Blue whisky ads over the years. They nailed the positioning with 'Men will be men'. No need for dialogue or even showing the product. Which is perfect given the surrogate advertising laws in India.

Seagram's Imperial Blue's 'Men will be men'

For Reckitt's condom brand Durex, we created a digital series inspired by a personal experience of mine. 'Sex Chat with Pappu and Papa' was the story of a 6-year-old boy who asks his dad the most embarrassing questions in public like, *"What is masturbation?", "Where do babies come from?", "Why do women bleed? From where do they bleed?"* And his dad's hilarious and heartfelt explanations. One of the first-ever fiction shows on sex education, we delivered it in 15 languages and it became one of the most viewed original shows on YouTube in India clocking upwards of 100mn views, and even schools use it for education. Talk about making an impact!

Sex Chat with Pappu and Papa, India's 1st sex-education fiction show

5. **Real:** The younger generation can smell bullshit from a mile away. They want the real deal, no filters, no posers. Authenticity is the name of the game. Brands that try to fake concern or put on a show usually end up face-first in a pile of memes. Remember Pepsi and Kendal Jenner? Yeah, not their finest moment. Great stories resonate because they're genuine, raw, and unapologetically themselves.

Today a brand needs to 'be', not pretend. Because they *will* get busted that way. The cliché of hiring or casting 'authentic looking people' always shows – the token man with a turban, a man in a skull cap and beard, another with a teeka to show secularity. Or showing 'youth' audiences with basketballs, colorful headphones... it's enough to make you want to throw up. It need not always be the dated definition of 'cool'. In Mere Dad ki Maruti, the characters were the kind of people you'd meet on a Roadies or Splitsvilla audition in Chandigarh. Rhea Chakraborty's character ["It's Jazzlin, not Jasleen!"] had a line that I'd actually heard in one of those, *"Main Chandigarh ki Shakira hoon!"* She wasn't your traditional 'Yash Raj Films heroine' with long hair, chiffon saree. Jazzlin was a fun, quirky girl with bad English and a twisted sense of humor. Which is what made her real. See even the gulabjamun uncle in Swiggy advertising – he has a fan following of his own!

Check out 'Always', with their #LikeAGirl campaign. They tackled the issue of girls' confidence during puberty head-on, redefining what it means to do something *"like a girl"* and empowering young women. It sparked conversations about gender stereotypes and made a real impact. That's the power of Branded Content with purpose!

Always campaign #LikeAGirl

Closer to home, P&G's detergent brand Ariel took on the issue of gender inequality in household chores and aimed to redefine traditional gender roles with its 'Share the Load' campaign. It struck a chord with audiences across India and beyond, challenging deep-rooted stereotypes. The campaign went on to pick up a ton of awards, generate loads of conversations and deliver impact for the brand.

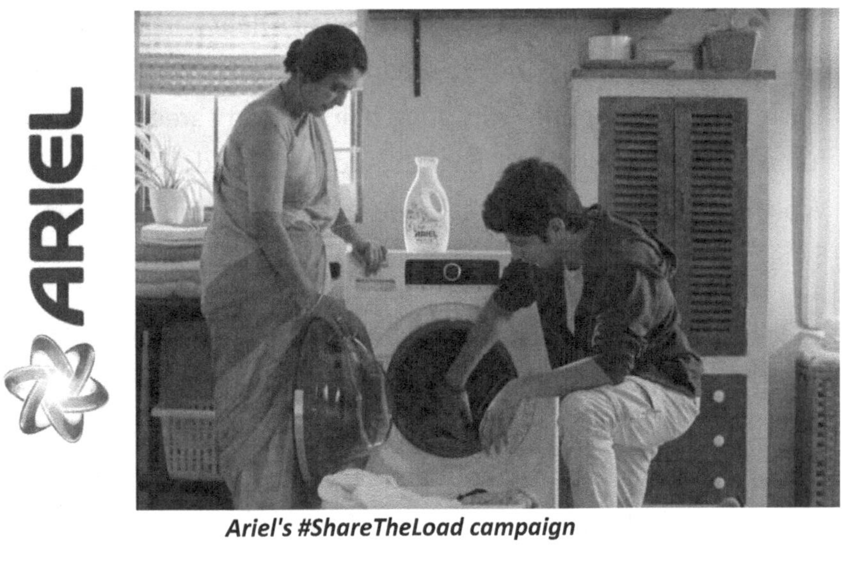

Ariel's #ShareTheLoad campaign

6. **Extendable:** You can't build muscle by doing one push-up, right? Same goes for building a lasting bond with your audience. You gotta tell multiple stories, like a snowball rolling down a mountain, gaining momentum and turning into an avalanche of awesomeness. Just look at the Marvel Universe. 22+ movies, US$22+ Billion. Bigger than Star Wars, James Bond, Harry Potter.

Remember BMW's 'The Hire' series? They started in 2001, and now they're back with Uma Thurman, Hans Zimmer, Sam Hargrave. It's like a cinematic reunion you don't wanna miss.

Vodafone's ZooZoos

And let's not forget the lovable Vodafone Zoo Zoos. Those weirdos kept us entertained with their antics for years.

7. **Timely:** Timing is everything in life, relationships and branded content. Just like in a relationship, you gotta progress from small talk to deep conversations at the right pace. No one wants to hear about your mom, or your ex on the first date, right? Well, the same goes for marketing and branded content.

Good stories are timely, they flow with the rhythm of the moment, capturing what matters to the audience.

When COVID-19 hit, Unilever's Lifebuoy handwash had a topical, **timely** campaign reminding us to wash our hands frequently, they do a **seasonal** campaign for kids to maintain hygiene after play during the rains when germs are in overdrive. But their **evergreen**, year-round communication is to always wash hands before/after meals, after visiting the toilet.

Now, one brand you cannot ignore if you're talking about iconic content and communication, is Apple. Remember their 'The Underdogs' series?

They released a topical WFH version during the lockdown, capturing the reality of our lives with humor: Search 'The whole working from home thing | Apple at work'.

There's their epic **seasonal** Christmas commercial in 2013 featuring a 'Misunderstood' teen. Search 'Apple Holiday ad, Misunderstood teen'.

And the **evergreen** – 'I'm the Greatest' film – one of those films you wish you'd made. Featuring a bunch of people going about their lives, getting dressed, dancing, singing, spending time with their kids, playing sports, playing music, hanging with friends, and more. They just happen to be disabled. Search 'Apple, The Greatest'.

8. **Make 'Em Care:** This generation is woke, folks. The guardians of the galaxy's conscience, fighting for what's right. Brands need to step up and join the cause. Purpose is a much-abused and a very confused term in marketing with absurd women's day ads and cakes from HR at work among other things. But brands do need to find purpose.

Products or services may not have opinions, but brands *need* to. What a brand stands for massively influences where consumers invest, who they work for and what they buy.

Given that there are no global governments, but there are global brands, this is not just a privilege but also a responsibility for branded content.

'Evan' for Sandy Hook Promise on one of the most important issues, especially in the US, simply blew my mind. No spoilers, just watch it. Thank me later. Search 'Evan, Sandy Hook Promise'.

In India, the 6-Pack Band campaign with Unilever's Brooke Bond Red Label tea is a great example. The brand is positioned as a social lubricant that encourages breaking social barriers one cup of tea at a time. The 6-Pack Band was India's first transgender band that did this one song at a time. Celebrating LGBTQ rights, shattering stereotypes. It went on to win India's first Cannes Grand Prix Glass Lion. More on this in a case study later.

These 8 are some of the key elements in telling a great story. But as we said, this is not just any story, it's a branded one. And integrating the brand smartly is critical for it to qualify as a great Branded Content story.

Elements to Evaluate the Branding Quotient

1. **Integration of Brand theme/ idea:** Back in the day, we used to joke about clients always saying, "Make the logo bigger!" But now, the real deal is making the idea bigger. You need that thematic tie-in with the core premise and promise of the brand. Take the 6-Pack Band and Brooke Bond Red Label, breaking social barriers over a cup of tea or a song. Or think about Red Bull and its promise of energy and an adrenaline rush in everything they do.

2. **Integration of Brand:** Beyond just the brand's themes. Brands need to figure how to bring something unique to the table. Something only, they can. For instance, for Red Bull it's their expertise in Extreme Sports, and The Lego Movie wouldn't exist without those iconic blocks and characters.

3. **Integration of Product/ Service:** If you can actively incorporate the usage or consumption of the product or service into the story, it strengthens the association. The BMW car is a key player in 'The Hire' series, and Marriot properties are essential in their Branded Content. Just look at Apple products in 'The Underdogs' series. From the first 'Escape from Office' to the follow-ups – they did it so well, without screaming "PRODUCT PLUG!"

Apple's 'The Underdogs' series

4. **Integration of Brand's benefit:** If you can cleverly weave in the primary benefit of the product, it adds an extra punch to the Branded Content. Remember Old Spice's, 'The Man Your Man Could Smell Like'? It promised to make your man smell more desirable, transforming him from average man to confident and attractive.

5. **Integration of attribute, feature:** Ideally, the benefit and the attribute/ feature go hand in hand. But sometimes, it's fun to integrate just the feature in content. Take Blendtec's Will It Blend?' series, where their founder, Tom Dickson, blended all sorts of unconventional items, from iPhones and golf balls to even iPads and glow sticks. It effectively demonstrated the blender's power, durability and performance.

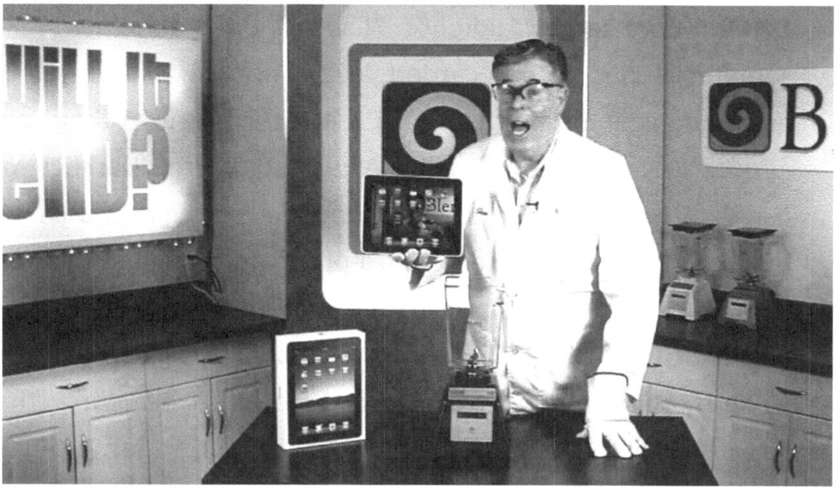

Blendtec's 'Will It Blend?' turning an iPad to putty

6. **Integration of Logo, Brand name, Tagline:** Ok, marketing people, relax! While just a generic placement of the logo or tagline won't cut it, there is no denying the benefit of doing that seamlessly in a relevant manner. Having the brand in the title of the Branded Content certainly helps not just branding, and association but media pick-up, and consumer engagement too. Like Coke Studio, Red Bull Stratos, Mere Dad ki Maruti, Ranveer Ching Returns. Yeah, they all benefited from that. You have no choice but to mention the brand when talking about the content.

Zomato did a great job recently kicking off an entire debate on the correct pronunciation of its brand name. They even went as far as changing the brand name to Mazoto instead of just playing up ZoMAto for a hilarious Mother's Day campaign.

Similarly, the tagline when smartly used can be really powerful and there are tons of examples of Nike's iconic 'Just Do It'.

7. **Fit with Core Target Audience:** Now this one's quite basic, but sometimes people get carried away with ideas or celebrity associations and forget to check if it resonates with their own core target audience. Like that Alia Bhatt starrer 'Darlings' on Netflix – her character is a lower middle-class girl in a chawl, but she's shown using some ultra-premium cosmetics, hair oil. It probably did more harm to the brand than the character's authenticity. Ouch! Pepsi used to be known to pick up the right celebrity before he or she exploded. They've done that historically with Shahrukh Khan, Sachin Tendulkar, Saif Ali Khan, Ranbir Kapoor. But when they started signing on celebrities who were 55+ and had been on 4 other beverage brands including competition and one from their own portfolio, it just baffled me! But then, the cola category is a weird one where this game of musical chairs happens all the time.

8. **Quality of Execution:** Now, if it's just some random piece of content, quality isn't always the be-all and end-all. Seriously, you could film it on a potato phone and it could still go viral. Look at all those cat videos and babies losing their mind over weird food. But when a brand jumps in, well, execution quality matters. Big time.

When Ching's decided to launch in the Bhojpuri market, they said in their signature style, *"Screw traditional commercials!"* [They said it in Hindi and it sounds far more colorful. God bless you, Ajay Gupta!] They went all-in on Branded Content. We hired the local singing superstar, Akshara Singh, and cooked up a spicy-hot song and music video about their Schezwan Chutney calling it 'Rocket Jawaani' – inspired by their tagline, 'Yeh chutney nahi, rocket hai rocket!' Now, most Bhojpuri music videos are produced on a shoestring budget. And it shows. They still do millions and millions of views. But the minute Ching's came into the mix, we had to step it up. We pulled in some fun names from the Bollywood world as composers, choreographers but retained the raunchiness of Bhojpuri music. We knocked off the overt double entendres that Bhojpuri music typically has, but retained the naughtiness and spice that went with the brand. The song set the market on fire, creating a massive trade pull, launching the brand with big impact.

Ching's 'Rocket Jawaani' with Akshara Singh

9. **Fit with Tone, Vibe, Feel:** Brands need to do the heavy lifting first and set a tone, establish a vibe. You know you've made it when your sound becomes an adjective. When someone says, *"That track has a Coke Studio type of sound."* Or they're like, *"Man, that ad had that Red Bull vibe, you know?"* All candid camera pranks were 'Bakra' based on the show we did at MTV. All spoofs and parodies were 'Fully Faltoo'.

Then you can get away without even showing the product, the logo, or the tagline. Take Nike with its swoosh. Imperial Blue only needs its ghazal track in the background. Most recently, Liquid Death has done that so well.

But hold up! Let's not forget that a mismatch in tone can be a total brand disaster. Imagine your favorite digital influencer starts dropping F-bombs left and right, and suddenly a family-friendly brand joins the chaos. Talk about a misfit! So, when creating Branded Content, stay true to your brand's tone and style. It need not be restrictive or stuck in a loop. Keep it consistent. That way, consumers can spot your brand from a mile away.

10. **Delivery against Brief/ Objectives:** Sure, the content might be a riot and blend the brand seamlessly, but if it doesn't hit the objectives, well, we've got a problem. It's like trying to have an amazing party with no food or music. You gotta be clear on your objectives from the get-go. If the goal is to drive traffic to a website, but your content takes a detour and starts doing something else entirely, time for a course-correction. You feel me?

Of course, you do need to note that Branded Content objectives are more medium to long-term, linked more to building trust, a bond with consumers and more vs. specific, immediate ones like lead generation.

11. **Legal & Ethical considerations:** This is where things can get messy. Brands gotta be extra careful these days when anything can offend anyone. We've got some basics to keep in mind.

A. **Copyright infringement:** No stealing other people's music, images, clips or any assets. That thing that if you use less than 5 seconds, it's ok? Wrong! Like seriously, you can't even use someone who sounds like Amitabh Bachchan without his permission anymore. The man copyrighted his voice!

B. **Disclosures and disclaimers:** Let's be honest, transparency is sexy. When you've got paid partnerships with influencers, tests conducted, or claims made, spill the beans. The Advertising Standards Councils of India, aka ASCI even has guidelines for this. So, no hiding in the shadows. Shine that light!

C. **Endorsements and testimonials:** When it comes to endorsements and testimonials, be it from celebrities or experts, make sure you have all the paperwork in order. I mean, seriously, don't pull a Sleepy Owl and Surreal Cereals move, thinking you can use lookalikes or people with similar names. That's just asking for trouble. It may save you legally, but the internet will eat you alive. This happened recently also to an edtech company that used Sundar Pichai's likeness for an ad.

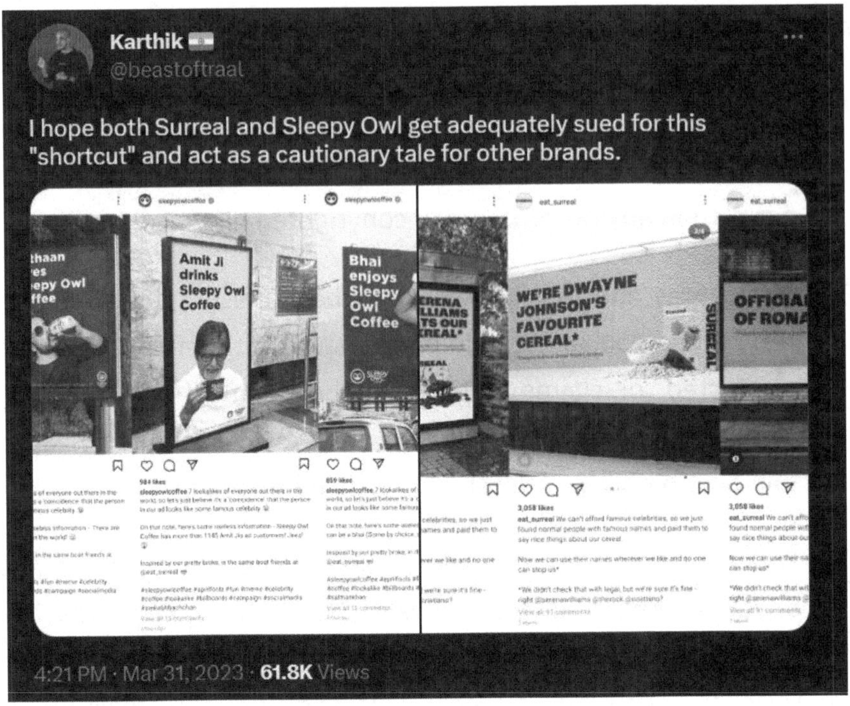

And hey, the same applies for bodies, organizations you quote or reference. Don't just put a man in a doctor's coat without proof. Give credit where credit is due, people!

D. **Kids and animals:** Ah, the little ones and our furry friends. We've got rules, laws and permissions to protect them. When working with minors and animals, follow those guidelines. Safety first, working hours and more.

E. **Cultural sensitivities:** This is a minefield. Religion and politics are like those sensitive topics at dinner. But the whole internet is at the table. In India, with all its diversity, it's even trickier. Some brands have had to backpedal and withdraw content because of the backlash. Tanishq, Brooke Bond Red Label and even Zomato recently learned that the hard way. They had good intentions, but if you mishandle it, boom! Backfire.

F. **Privacy concerns:** No one wants their personal data floating around like a lost sock in the dryer. When it comes to brands, they need to step up and handle personal data in a responsible and ethical manner. No funny business, and any data collection needs to be in compliance with relevant laws and regulations.

G. **Regulatory compliances:** Some categories have mandatory call-outs. We're talking about mutual funds, gaming, betting, tobacco, alcohol, and more. Legal drinking age call-outs, addiction warnings, statutory health disclaimers, added flavors – yeah, they've got specific guidelines for each, with details on point size, duration on screen and more. So, study those guidelines and don't accidently stumble into a regulatory mess.

So, there's your checklist to evaluate the entertainment and branding quotient of your content. Now, don't go checking off every box like a robot. We don't want a formulaic snooze fest. And remember, this isn't a comprehensive list. But if you're hitting only a 10% of these, it's time to probably go back to the drawing table.

Checklist for evaluation

Sr.	Entertainment	Sr.	Branding
1.	Relatability	1.	Idea/ Theme
2.	Novelty	2.	Brand
3.	Conflict	3.	Product/ Service
4	Simplicity	4.	Benefit
5.	Authenticity	5.	Attribute/ Feature
6.	Extendable	6.	Logo/ Brand name/ Tagline
7.	Timely	7.	Fit with Target Audience
8.	Makes me care	8.	Quality of Execution
		9.	Fit with Tone/ Vibe
		10.	Delivery against brief
		11.	Legal, ethical considerations

Download the checklist at BrandedContentBoss.com/resources

But, here's the deal, after all the brainstorming, the epic writing, the kick-ass production, and checking off those boxes... in the end, it all comes down to one thing: Did it make me feel?

WRITING A GREAT BRANDED CONTENT BRIEF

This is the starting point for all creative work. Be it for traditional advertising or Branded Content. And a great, inspiring brief is key to cracking the right idea. Now, I've seen my fair share of briefs, and unfortunately, some people really know how to cock it up. I once got a brief in my early advertising days that basically said, *"Hey, write any headline you want as long as it has the following words in it: Long, Shiny, Black, Luxurious, Hair."* [Kaaley ghanney, lambey baal.] Talk about a creativity killer.

A brief should be a springboard, not a shackle for the creative team. You want enough information to set the context, understand the business and marketing objectives, identify the target audience, and of course, grasp the brand's unique vibe. But let's not drown in data, okay? Let's keep it concise, snappy and exciting... remember it's called 'brief'.

Now, personally, I'm the kind of guy who likes to dive deep. I'll immerse myself in a sea of information, data, insights, reports, you name it. I'll even have a chat with some consumers and trade folks to get the inside scoop. But hey, we're all different. Some of you might have a different process, and that's cool too.

That being said, there are a few key elements that you should capture in your creative brief. It's a lot like a creative or communication brief, but with a few spicy twists. Think of it as a remix, if you will.

BRANDED CONTENT BRIEF TEMPLATE		
Sr.	**Content**	**Details**
1.	*Client name	Name of the Parent company.
2.	*Brand name	The particular brand for which this brief is.
3.	*Product/ service category	The category in which the brand operates, e.g.: FMCG, packaged foods, automobiles, two-wheelers, financial services, etc.
4.	*Product details	Range of flavors, variants, sizes, models, price range, colors available, USP, other information that may be useful.

		What is it, what does it do? What distinguishes it or makes it special? What are the benefits of it's key features?
5.	*Link to brand's communication	TVC, print, outdoor ads, any influencer campaigns, press releases and other communication created. Any legacy work to be shared. Helps give a sense of tone, style. Any thing in the brand's history that can be used, told?
6.	*Link to social media pages/ handles	May help give a sense of tone, style, personality, any recurring themes, if these have been well-managed. Would also give a sense of consumer reactions, kind of engagement, comments. Instagram, Facebook, YouTube, Twitter, LinkedIn, Discord, Snapchat, Tik Tok [if relevant], Website, other.
7.	*Tagline	Any key slogans, lines being used, e.g.: Nike's Just Do it, Pepsi's Rise Up Baby. If this is up for review, is to be changed or not to be touched, it's important to indicate that as well.
8.	*Brand ambassadors, celebrity associations, mascots, experts	If there have been any endorsement campaigns, or any industry experts used. Any mascots, like the Amul girl or so who need to be incorporated, details, images, references. Similarly, are there any influencers who impact this particular category? Tech gurus, chefs, other? This may fuel ideas for collaborations or using them as media channels.

9.	*Target audience	Bull's eye audience... Demographics Psychographic profile But go beyond and ideally paint a bit of a picture. Who is this person? What does he/ she do? For fun, for entertainment? Where? What do they like to consume, watch? What do they want to do? Looking for a shortcut to save time? Want to upskill? What are their dreams, aspirations? And how does the brand enable this, or fit in? Is there a split on primary vs. secondary audience? Is there an existing community that's a source for content, feedback, ideas? The media/ platforms where the audience spends time? Does this impact the format of your solution/ content?
10.	*Priority markets	If there's a skew to metros, or tier 1? Besides impacting the eventual distribution, it may also influence the tone and content. You may choose to go a lot more Hindi vs. English or cast/ write characters accordingly.
11.	*Marketing objectives	At a larger, thematic level, what business problem is marketing trying to solve? Is it building awareness, driving sampling, attempting to bring in new audiences, opening new markets, repositioning the brand a little younger? This is one of the most important elements of this brief as it moves the

		conversation away from just a 'key message' – given that the creative solution may not even be a 'message'. It could be a program, an action.
12.	*Campaign objectives	Drill down to more specifics on this particular campaign, content. What do you hope to achieve? Drive subscriptions? Drive engagement? Other?
13.	Competition	What is the competitive framework that the brand operates in? Core category or broader things it competes with? Key competitors? Their advantages, differences?
14.	*Key messages for this campaign	What is the one thing that you wish to communicate through this?
15.	*Target timelines	Key dates like launch date and if there are longer approval processes, then to plan for that.
16.	*Budget range	Now, most people tend to leave this blank, or give the worst possible replies like "Need-based" or "Budget is not a problem". Then creative guys create the plan for a Rolls Royce, the budget available is for a Maruti 800. Wastes everyone's time. Set aside the media budget, but indicate a range or zone at least. And you're free to indicate that if the idea is compelling enough that you'd be happy to revisit the numbers.
17.	Mandatories, if any	Legal call-outs in case of surrogate ads, work in financial services, things like 'exclude kids, cuss words'. Any specifics like usage of brand sting

		to sign off [Britannia's ting ting ta ting audio mnemonic, Netflix's Tudum], a mascot. Pronunciations. When we did some Hyundai product films, everyone had a different pronunciation for the brand name! So, it was critical to align and educate the crew before the consumer!
18.	Metrics to measure success	How will this campaign be evaluated? Watch time, views, engagement, other?
19.	*Briefing date	When the brief is being delivered. The person should mail, offer to also talk the team through it for clarifications if necessary.
20.	*Expected turnaround date for 1st cut idea, proposal	Linked to launch dates, working backwards for approvals, prep, production, pre-marketing and more.
21.	Any other info that may be useful	Research studies, reports, consumer data, profiles, international campaigns the client has liked, past brand associations that worked well.

The brief writing and receiving process should be formally documented. The intent is not to make it bureaucratic, but to add a sense of seriousness. It also helps hold people accountable on the input and output.

Briefed by:	**Brief approved by:**
Name and designation of person writing the brief. Should be someone with reasonable authority, decision making power.	Name and designation of person they report to. Ideally a senior person depending on scale, budget of campaign.
Date:	**Date:**
Brief received by:	**Confirmed by:**
Name and designation of team lead/ person receiving the brief.	The person they report to.
Date:	**Date:**

*Mandatory fields to be filled.

Download blank templates to use at
BrandedContentBoss.com/resources

So, there you have it. The essentials of writing a kickass branded content brief.

It starts off like a mild-mannered creative brief for advertising in the classic format, but slowly rips open its shirt to reveal the superhero suit, cape and all underneath... for a Branded Content piece.

Remember, keep it brief, keep it exciting, and for the love of all things long, shiny and black, don't stifle that creativity.

Now go forth and create something that'll blow our minds!

INTEGRATING IN EXISTING VS. CREATING FRESH BRANDED CONTENT

Ah, the clash of the titans: integrating a brand in existing content vs. creating fresh Branded Content. Now, these are two different approaches altogether. It's like hiring a swanky club for a bash or hosting a party at your own pad. Both have their pros and pitfalls. Let's dig into some, shall we?

Upsides of Integrating in Existing Content

- **Existing audience:** When you piggyback on an established property, you're tapping into a ready-made fanbase. It's like arriving at a party when it's already in full swing. Take the IPL, it's got millions of eyeballs glued to their screens. Talk about a captive audience!

- **Larger scale:** Sometimes, an existing property has a scale that you couldn't even dream of replicating. Imagine Ray-Ban trying to create a Top Gun with Tom Cruise independently. It'd be like trying to wrestle a grizzly bear with a toothpick. But hey, that product placement with Maverick wearing their shades? Genius move that sold Aviators like hotcakes!

- **Greater Cost-efficiency:** Existing content comes with production efficiencies that a one-off creation can only dream of. It's like ordering in bulk instead of individually crafted masterpieces. Of course, if the integrations cost you an arm, a leg, and your firstborn, then maybe it's time to rethink.

- **Credibility rub-off:** When you hitch your brand to a massive content property or influencer, you ride the wave of their credibility. It's like showing up to a high-end fashion event with the A-listers. Suddenly, you're rubbing shoulders with luxury. Not too shabby, right?

Downsides of Integrating in Existing Content

- **Limited Creative Control:** When it's someone else's property, you're not calling all the shots. They hold the power to decide what flies and what crashes. So, your say in how your brand is represented might be as limited as a diet soda at a burger joint. Not ideal.

- **Clutter conundrum:** Existing content can sometimes be a branding battleground. Take the IPL again. With logos plastered on team jerseys and more sponsors than you can count, it's a jungle out there. I have no recollection whatsoever of the different sponsors of those Best Catches/ Super Sixes. You don't want to fade into the background like a chameleon with a branding crisis.

- **Audience backlash:** If you mess it up, oh boy, brace yourself for the wrath of the loyal fans. They can turn on your brand faster than a caffeinated squirrel on roller-skates. Nobody likes a sell-out, so be careful not to upset the delicate balance of content and consumer loyalty.

- **Controversy and negative associations:** Remember that Coca-Cola fiasco with Ronaldo? Yeah, that's the kind of mess you want to avoid. Celebrities endorsing things they don't use, or being caught in contradictions. A vegan plugging chicken wings! The same can happen with events and content as well. You don't want to be caught with your branding pants down.

- **Price escalations:** Success comes with a price tag. If the property you hitched your wagon to becomes a roaring success, they might demand a bigger investment from you. And if you can't keep up, well, a competitor very well could.

Upsides of Creating Fresh Branded Content

- **Total creative control:** You're the boss, the creative genius behind the wheel. You get to call all the shots, not just for your brand but also for the content. It's like having your own personal playground where you can unleash your wildest ideas.

- **Zero clutter:** Imagine a pristine landscape where your brand is the shining star, with no annoying competitors or even any other pesky brands stealing the spotlight. It's like being the only hero in a comic book universe. No capes required.

- **More hard-working:** Existing content could have its own set of objectives and agendas, but freshly created Branded Content is like a loyal sidekick, dedicated solely to serving your brand's objectives. It's like having a trusty companion who always has your back and works tirelessly to make you shine and it could work harder for your brand.

- **Ownership of IP:** The existing idea always belongs to someone else. But when you create something from scratch, it's yours, baby! You have the power to squeeze every drop of potential from your idea. Scale it up, extend it in wild ways, and even monetize it by partnering with other brands, platforms if it finds enough traction. It's like owning a magical unicorn that poops gold. Well, metaphorically speaking.

Downsides of Creating Fresh Branded Content

- **Limited audience:** Unless you crack the code on a killer distribution idea or partner with a big platform, the reach of your freshly minted Branded Content might be limited. You're starting from ground-up, building your empire brick by brick. The parallel of hosting a party in a hidden location and hoping people show up when you've not given them the location pin... which may restrict the reach you finally get for the content.

- **Limited budgets, more expensive:** Creating fresh content means carving out a budget from your marketing/ advertising funds. You're playing with a finite number, unlike established properties that already have big bucks flowing in. You can't build a luxury yacht with pocket change.

- **Uncertainty of success:** Entertainment is a fickle beast. Ask me. With a fresh idea, there's always the risk of it vanishing into thin air, like a magician's disappearing act gone wrong. But hey, that's the thrill of the game. It's like playing Russian roulette with unicorns. Exciting, yet potentially dangerous.

- **Lack of domain expertise in entertainment:** Look, you're a master in your own business category, but diving into the entertainment realm is a whole new ballgame. Even with expert help, your limited understanding of the industry can be a speed bump on the road to success. Like you can't win a dance-off without knowing how to do the Macarena!

But remember, it's not an either/ or scenario. You can mix and match these approaches to find your perfect blend. Start by partnering with existing properties, dip your toes into fresh content with smaller ideas, and eventually go all-in with a hero concept. It can be a hybrid approach. But your marketing objectives, ambitions, budgets will help decide the right mix. The key is to start the party, my friends.

HOW TO WORK WITH PARTNERS TO CREATE BRANDED CONTENT

Irrespective of whether you're integrating a brand into existing content or creating Branded Content from scratch, you can't fly solo. It's like trying to win a dance-off with two left feet. You need some back up, and that means partnering with the right peeps. But, one of the biggest blunders people make is hiring an expert and then telling them what to do. Seriously, that's like ordering a gourmet meal and then asking the chef to make it taste like a microwave dinner. Let the pros do their thing.

Tips to extract greatness from your creative partners when diving into Branded Content

1. **Clarity of Brief:** First things first, you gotta have a clear vision, expectations, brand tone, and all that jazz. It's like cracking a good joke – if you don't know the punchline, nobody's gonna laugh. And hey, brands, you better do your homework and know yourselves before you start this process. Ain't no AI or ChatGPT gonna magically figure it out for you. Get your act together.

2. **Cast the Right Team:** Working with the right people is crucial. It's not always about hiring the most expensive or popular folks out there. Don't just stand next to the most popular kid in the room, because they might not be the right fit. I've seen it happen, people try to save a few bucks by hiring the wrong team, or spend a bomb on the current hottie who's not really as excited and guess what? They end up spending twice as much fixing the mess. Sometimes, a fresh mind with a hunger for success can bring a whole new flavor to the table. Sometimes, you may find the right partner in a completely different category altogether. So, review their understanding of the brief, track record, experience, hunger, passion, vibe, and of course, their budget. Make a smart call, and you might be pleasantly surprised.

   For a lot of the Ching's Desi Chinese content, we pulled Bollywood directors who had never directed a commercial before – like Rohit Shetty, Shaad Ali, Maneesh Sharma, Ali Abbas Zafar – but had a great handle on entertainment, storytelling at scale and connecting with mass audiences. The balance came in with us ensuring the brand guardrails were in place, and they surprised us with the impact they delivered. For the first time, we heard a client say, *"Hey, this may be too in-your-face, can we tone down the branding?"*.

3. **Give them Space:** Once you have a sharp brief, brand guardrails in place, step back and let the magic happen. Don't be a micro-manager, obsessing over the color of the t-shirt or the paint on the walls. You gotta give these creative geniuses the elbow room they need to work their magic. Trust me, it's the only way to make sparks fly.

4. **Take Some Risks:** Playing it safe is the riskiest thing you can do in this game. With all the content clutter out there, you'll get lost like a puppy without a leash at the Kumbh Mela. You gotta push boundaries, try new formats, genres, casting choices, crew and more. It'd be nuts to keep doing the same thing and expect different results, no? Most government organizations had not tried a song/ music video as a Public Safety Announcement. So when 'Dumb Ways to Die' landed as a Melbourne Safety promo it was a huge clutter-breaker. A 5-minute short film to sell noodles and condiments in a dystopian world that also cost a fair share of the marketing budget required balls of steel if Manchurian balls had to sell and 'Ranveer Ching Returns' sure demonstrated it was worth it!

5. **Prep for Success:** Most people plan for failure, but not many plan for success. It's like they can't even imagine it. Well, take a page from Marvel's book. They design stories and characters that go beyond a single film. They create entire universes where crossovers happen, and fans go wild. Of course, a sequel

happens only if the original is successful, but it needs to be thought through that way. So, think beyond the first hit. If your content strikes gold, be ready to expand, extend and surprise your audience. Remember, James Brand will return!

6. **Be Patient:** Branded Content ain't no sprint. It's a damn marathon. It takes time to build that unshakeable bond with your audience. So don't expect overnight success. But I've seen it work across the board, across categories. It's a slow burn, but the payoff is worth it. Stick with it, and you'll reap the rewards.

7. **Keep At It:** Just like you can't get a 6-pack from 1 push-up, if you're going to do a one-off standalone piece of Branded Content and wait for consumers to pour in, you've got another thing coming. You will need to consistently stay at it to build muscle, to get fit, to build that bond with your audience. It's like going to the gym, but instead of lifting weights, you're lifting the spirits of your customers.

Related side-note, be wary of any team pitching you a campaign vs. a program. Remember Branded Content and content marketing are not a tactical campaign, it's an approach.

Now, lock these tips in your brain vault as you dive into the creative abyss with your partners. May the Entertainment Gods be ever in your favor.

One watch-out: there are some folks who get all weak in the knees when they work with experts, celebrities or heavyweights. They clam up and then end up cursing the job done. Remember this, while the creative partners may be the masters of entertainment and content, nobody knows your brand better than you do. So, it's ok to put on your big boy or big girl pants and stand up for your brand and it's needs. You can be polite, yet firm, and strike that perfect balance.

Tips to share feedback with creative partners for Branded Content like a pro

1. **HOW you give feedback is AS important as what feedback you give:** If you come across as overly critical and mean, those poor souls on the receiving end might just shut down completely. Then even if your feedback is pure gold, it's useless if they can't handle it. Now, I'm not saying you should sugar-coat things with a load of bullshit. But a little sugar does help make swallowing a bitter pill easier. Catch my drift?

2. **Start with the positives:** Always. Find something good to say, even if you're dealing with the worst scripts known to mankind. Frame your criticisms in a positive, constructive light. Look, if someone managed to complete a full-fledged series script, a goddamn 100 pages or even a book – no matter how shitty – that is something! Most people can't get past writing a damn email. That in itself is a friggin' achievement. There may be a scene, a line, a character, a turn of phrase, or if nothing else, their passion to do this. Something that you can appreciate. And you must!

3. **When giving suggestions, give choices:** And call out that these are suggestions only and they will probably have better ideas. Even KBC ['Who wants to be a millionaire?'] gives you four

options, for crying out loud. Position your ideas as, *"Hey, here's a random idea, but I know you'll probably blow it out of the water with something better. This is just to get you thinking about how you could possibly fix this or try something else?"* – Put the creator/ writer back in the driver's seat again. Give them options to explore instead of forcing your way down their throats.

4. **Communicate that this is NOT personal:** Let them know that your feedback is all about the Branded Content piece, not a judgment on their writing skills [although, let's be honest, you might have a few notes on that too]. It's part of a collaborative learning process. Most writers understand that all writing is re-writing. Every damn word of it. Creating Branded Content is a team effort, from the writing stage all the way to casting, production, scoring, editing, and even promotion. We're all in this together, baby!

5. **Don't get stuck on your own feedback:** I've seen it happen before. People fall head over heels in love with their own precious feedback, and it's a recipe for disaster. Sure, share it, push it, defend it, but be open to being convinced otherwise. If those creative partners have some compelling counters to your notes, be humble enough to consider them. It's a collaboration, not a one-man show.

6. **Be Specific:** For the love of all things holy. *"Mazaa nahi aaya"/ "Issmein woh nahi" ["It's not fun"/"It doesn't have zing!"]* is as useful as a screen door on a submarine. When sharing feedback, don't be a vague mess. Tell them what ain't working. Is it the conflict or the lack of it? The setting? The tone? The

climax? The timing of that oh-so-important brand placement? The choice of music? Get down to specifics. Make your feedback actionable. What will help? What needs to be shortened? What's missing a beat? Should they introduce a new element to spice things up? Do the dialogues need a punch up? Maybe another layer of conflict would do the trick? Raising the stakes? And don't forget the practicalities of production. Does this look affordable/ on-budget? Or is it starting with a shot of the Taj Mahal blowing up? Are there any mandatories to be ring-fenced about the brand? If you don't do all that, your feedback will be as bland as a tofu sandwich at a steakhouse. It won't have that magical 'zing' we're looking for.

Now, let's flip sides to look at this from a Creator's perspective.

Remember being profitable is what gives us the privilege to be creative. And Branded Content is like a golden ticket to tell great stories with someone else's money. And with great stories told with someone else's money comes even greater responsibility!

Just as a brand can choose to get integrated/ partner with some existing content or create something from scratch, as a creator, there are two approaches to strike these partnerships for creators.

1. **Pull the Brand:** So, you're already a big shot with a massive following, a track record, and suddenly a brand or agency comes knocking on your door, wanting to partner up. They're either interested in your existing ideas or they want your help to create something from scratch with them.

2. **Push for the Brand:** Now, maybe you're new to the game or even if you're a seasoned pro, there's that one brand that gets you all excited. Or it's a potential new revenue source for you and you proactively reach out to a brand or their agency pitching your existing ideas or proposing to build something entirely new.

The notes on evaluating great entertainment and branding apply to you as well as you think through the idea, it's execution and final delivery, distribution.

You can look at the popular trade e-zines where new campaigns get covered, and LinkedIn of course, to create a hitlist of brands, marketers, agencies to go after. Identify, pitch, rinse and repeat. Once you deliver on some content, you may become the go-to-choice, so don't hesitate.

Brass tacks for Creators to deliver kickass Branded Content

1. **Understand the Brand and the Brief:** Sure, it's the brand's responsibility to provide clear and adequate information, but it's also on you to fully grasp their essence, their brand and the brief. Don't be shy to ask questions, asking them to fill in the blanks if there's information missing, and to immerse yourself in the category, the audience and more. That is what will help you create Branded Content that resonates with the brand's values and speaks to both their audience and yours.

2. **Tell a Great Story, Well:** Your expertise in Content is what they're after. No matter how slick the integration or brand

placement, if the content doesn't entertain, it's all a waste of time. And neither will the brand come back, nor will your audience. Be real, be authentic, be honest. But most of all, be entertaining!

3. **Collaborate with the Brand:** Money talks, and in most cases for Branded Content, that money comes from the brand. Some of my best creative work has happened when I've collaborated with brands that pushed me to do better. So don't fight them. Understand their needs and objectives, and make sure the content helps them achieve their goals.

4. **Stand Up to Them:** Collaborating doesn't mean being a push-over. A lot of new creators who are just starting out, young agencies or even established ones that are heavily dependent on a brand's money are scared of pushing back on notes or feedback that compromises the content. Some don't do it out of fear, some out of habit, some out of not caring enough. Well, snap out of it! The brand may know their brand best, but they came to you because you know how to entertain better than them. If something they say doesn't make sense, explain it to them constructively, with alternative solutions or strong logic. Most reasonable clients [yes, they do exist] will see your point of view and agree. And if they don't, don't be afraid to walk away.

5. **Transparency, Tracking & More:** Sometimes those briefs and partnerships come with additional asks. Influencers, for example, aren't just about their personality and content, but also their distribution and audience. For platforms, there'll be deliverables for views, impressions and all that other good stuff.

If you can align on the objectives, and manage expectations up ahead, and proactively share insights, not just data on what worked, what could have been done better, you'll build trust with the brand.

6. **Clarity of Communication:** Sometimes, our brilliant ideas get lost in the Bermuda Triangle of miscommunication because they've not been explained, presented well. Typically, no one better than the person who originally conceived the idea to present it. But not every writer or director is a good presenter. When evaluating film scripts, I usually prefer a read so I can evaluate the idea on its own merit without the smoke and mirror of the narration. But then some ideas need a little extra love. You gotta sprinkle in some references, examples, and maybe even a magic trick or two. The goal is to help the brand evaluate your idea correctly and not throw the baby out with the bathwater. Oh, and don't forget to prepare, rehearse, and if need be, even script that pitch of yours as well and do a mock Q&A. If you spent a week cracking the idea, ensuring it's presented/ pitched right is as important as your morning coffee.

   Now, drumroll please, I present to you a template of sorts for your idea/ proposal. Consider it a friendly guide to make sure you cover all the key elements. It's your torch in the dark, not a leash to stifle your creativity. So, grab that PowerPoint presentation, whip up a snazzy Canva deck, or keep it simple with a good ol' Word document. Heck, you can even go wild and create a video pitch. The format doesn't matter as long as you have a written document that's not just useful, but downright essential to be able to go back to, review. Don't mistake the sizzle for the steak. Let's light up that proposal and knock 'em off their feet.

Template to present creative idea for Branded Content

BRANDED CONTENT PROPOSAL TEMPLATE		
Sr.	**Content**	**Details**
1.	*Client name	Name of Parent company.
2.	*Brand name	Brand under discussion.
3.	*Background & Brief	Snapshot of brief, objectives, timelines, budgets, key information. Key triggers that influence the idea being presented.
4.	*Title of Property	What are you calling it? It could be a working title. When kids don't get named for long, they land up with nicknames like Pappu, Pinky, Tinku, Munna & Munni. Aur Munni badnaam hi hoti hai!
5.	*Idea logline	Elevator pitch of the concept. If you can't pitch the idea in one line to the brand, chances are you won't be able to do that to your audience. For a general piece of entertainment, like a film for instance, a format to crack this is fill in the following blanks: "My story is a [genre, format] called [title] about [hero, lead] who wants [goal] despite [obstacle]." Now, for Branded Content, add... "... and how [brand] plays a role in helping him achieve that." For eg: "Mere Dad ki Maruti is a feature length comedy about a boy who sneaks out his stingy dad's new Maruti Ertiga to

		impress the college hottie and then loses the car! He must now encounter an over-eager car salesman, a car rental company run by a gun-toting geriatric, some dangerous car thieves and his dad to recover the car in time."
6.	*Idea details	Open up the idea a bit more. The consumer insight it's based on. What makes it unique. Details of the story, characters, segments. Genre/ Format/ Number of episodes, chapters/ Duration.
7.	Reference/ tone	Audio/ video/ image references you may need to showcase the idea, the treatment, the style, soundscape, energy.
8.	Potential talent associated	Recommendations on casting, key crew, options. Their names, profiles, past work, reason why you're recommending them.
9.	*Brand integration	Thematic fitment Title Logo, tagline integration, visually, verbally, other ways like signage, apparel Product/ service integrations, placements, usage, consumption Graphic integrations, any segment branding, etc. Any other integration, customization Other entitlements, exclusive content, etc. Tags on social media Spokesperson featured in making of videos, on media events Contests or more
10.	Marketing, promotions [optional]	If there are any PR, Social Media commitments, etc. If this requires a separate budget, mention that.

11.	Extension possibilities	This can be detailed later but it helps to outline the ways it can be spun-off… it gives the brand great line of sight on the potential of the idea and how it can grow. It could be in the form of Merchandise/ On-ground/ Ancillary content. And indicate if it's at incremental cost. If there's surround content being delivered as part of the core proposal then outline that.
12.	*Timelines	Clear next steps, responsibilities and deadlines, e.g.: Concept presentation/ Feedback/ Tweaks/ Budget presentation/ Discussion, approval/ Prep/ Production/ Post/ Promotion/ Go live date
13.	Deliverables/ Reach	Various assets you deliver in terms of units with ancillary content. Or depending on the structure of the deal, the impressions, views, engagement committed. Be mindful not to overpromise/underdeliver.
14.	*Budgets	Don't budget something without details as it can land you in a soup. But this is an expected question on ballpark costs. Have a broad handle or at least list out elements that need to be planned for: Cost of Production/ Talent Marketing/ Space/ Inventory/ Social-media/ Digital/ PR/ Project/ Creative fee. If any specific payment terms, advances, talent payments required upfront. In case of multiple sponsor pods, flag if the brand will be sharing space with another brand.
15.	*Proposal	Brands are in a hurry when the brief is

	validity	shared to get the idea but then take forever for feedback. Ideas pitched weeks ago may come back when no longer doable or relevant. So, keep a clear 4-to-6-week cut-off with deliverables to be reviewed, reconfirmed past that deadline.
16.	*Confiden-tiality	It is worthwhile to also add a footer on the proposal that the ideas being presented are both confidential and privileged. If an NDA needs to be shared, any script needs to be registered with relevant bodies, that may be worthwhile considering as well.

Just like the accountability for the brief and approvals, it's important to have a process for idea development, execution, closure too. And documenting the presentation is always a good idea for the same.

Proposal submitted by:	Confirmed by:
Name and designation of person driving, developing the idea.	Name and designation of person they report to. Ideally a senior person depending on scale, budget of campaign.
Date:	**Date:**

Proposal received by:	Confirmed by:
Ideally this should be the same team lead/ person who shared the brief.	The person they report to.
Date:	**Date:**

*Mandatory fields to be filled.
Download blank templates to use at
BrandedContentBoss.com/resources

Clear deadlines, responsibilities are essential to pin down expectations at both ends.

NEXT STEPS & TIMELINES		
Action	**Responsibility**	**Deadline**
Briefing	Brand	Day 01
Concept presentation	Creator	Day 08
Feedback	Brand	Day 12
Concept tweak, with budget presentation	Creator	Day 15
Concept, budget finalization	Brand + Creator	Day 20
Paperwork, advances	Brand + Creator	Day 24
Prep	Creator	Day 25 to Day 55
Final presentation with details, pre-execution	Creator	Day 56
Execution	Creator	Day 60 to Day 65
Post	Creator	Day 66 to 80
First cut presentation	Creator	Day 81
Feedback	Brand	Day 84
Tweak and final presentation	Creator	Day 90
Finalization	Brand + Creator	Day 92
Final deliveries, versions	Creator	Day 93 to Day 100
Final payments	Brand	Day 120

Marketers and creators, listen up! You're a dynamic duo, like peanut butter and jelly, Batman and Robin, or tequila and lime. You know you can't work without each other. And now you know how you can work with each other without gouging each other's eyeballs out.

Now that you're armed with wisdom I've bestowed upon you, it's time to join forces, stay alive, and create something truly kickass. A Branded Content campaign so legendary that I'll be quoting it in the next edition of my book. That's the level of awesomeness we're aiming for, my friends. Now go forth, my fearless warriors of creativity. Unleash your brilliance, entertain the masses and make Branded Content history together. And hey, when you do, make sure to save me a spot in the acknowledgements and your awards thank you speech.

LEAD TIMES FOR CREATING BRANDED CONTENT

Alright, hold on tight as we dive into the mysterious realm of lead times for creating Branded Content. While I understand that this is a key factor to plan your marketing calendar, product launches, but brace yourself for some uncertainties and variables.

Pinpointing exact timelines for different formats is like trying to catch a greased pig wearing roller skates. It's a wild ride, full of twists and turns. We've got factors like idea scale, complexity, creator speed, talent availability, approval processes, your cash-flows, and a whole bunch of other craziness thrown into the mix. It's a recipe for chaos, I tell you.

But fear not, let's attempt to shed some light on this chaotic dance. Keep in mind, though, that these are rough estimates, like trying to hit a dartboard with your hands tied behind your back. They don't account for the time you spend scribbling ideas, the endless back-and-forth of feedback, the soul-sucking bureaucracy that comes with it, and all the other administrative nightmares [vendor-registrations, three-quotations, contracts, advances... go ahead, kill me now] that haunt us. And oh, let's not forget the pre-launch marketing frenzy.

Here are some indicative ranges for execution, assuming a mid-range scale and decent quality, of course, once you've greenlit the idea and budget. A song and music video can take anywhere from two weeks to two months. I know, it's a wide gap, but life is full of surprises.

Broad lead times to execute different formats of Branded Content

Format	Execution time	Includes
Song/ audio [3 to 5 mins]	2 to 4 weeks	Writing the lyrics, composition of melody, recording the music and vocals, mix and mastering.

Music video [3 to 5 mins]	4 to 8 weeks	Prep including styling, art, choreography, location, rehearsals, actual shoot, edit, color correction, graphics, final master.
Talk-show, podcast [6 episodes, 30 to 40 mins]	8 to 10 weeks	Finalizing idea, format, host, guests, script/ question/ interview guide, set design, art, styling, shoot, edit, final master.
Reality show [6 episodes, 30 to 40 mins]	20 to 24 weeks	Finalizing idea, format, cast [would increase if an audition process as content is involved], recces, location blocks [assumed not too much travel, controlled set], shoot, edit, final master.
Fiction-show [5 episodes, 30 mins]	24 to 28 weeks	Finalizing story, screenplay, dialogues, casting, rehearsals, prep, shoot, edit, color correction, scoring music, title packaging, episodic promos, final master.
Feature film [100 to 120 min]	40 to 50 weeks	Finalizing idea, story, screenplay, dialogues, casting, prep, recces, rehearsals, styling, art, location [assuming not heavy action, VFX driven, and not too much outdoor, exterior], shoot, edit, scoring, dubs, sound clean-ups, color correction, final master.

Magazine, Journal, Book [100 pages]	10 to 12 weeks	Idea, writing out the content, stories, articles, adding in the pictures, illustrations [assumed no hectic photo shoots], design, layouts, proofing, cover design, printing [and not a very large print run, beyond a few thousand copies].
Tutorial videos	2 to 4 weeks	Planning, writing, prep, shoot, edit. Assumption is these are simpler cooking recipe, DIY, unboxing, FAQ answers and could even be graphic based.
Event [Not the IPL, IIFA or the Olympics which would take between 6 months, or 1 to 4 years to plan.]	10 to 12 weeks	Idea, design, planning, scripting, casting, set design, location booking, construction, rehearsals, tech-checks, lighting, sound, live execution, dismantling. Besides guest list planning, invites, etc.
Social media bank	1 to 4 weeks	Idea, writing, design… but, of course, agility of turn-arounds here would be essential to do things even in under an hour if required.

If we talk about formats like games, places like a full-fledged amusement park or experience centre [think Disneyland, House of Barbie, Lego Discovery Centre], the lead times could be far longer. Like a location/ place that you're building may involve identifying real estate, that whole negotiation, and the licenses, permissions involved could be a lot more complex besides the actual design, construction and more.

Now, obviously, these timelines can be crunched or may take substantially longer depending on the variables involved. But it's just to give a broad sense as you start planning out your marketing calendar. So, don't go whining about, *"But you promised it would take only 2 weeks!"* I've learned that life rarely goes according to plan.

Having a Branded Content/ Content Marketing Calendar is essential, but don't complicate your life and overfill it generating a GANTT chart that requires a scientist to help people decode it. It should be simple enough for everyone to be able to use it. You can have a few simple headers and sections working backwards that cover off the key milestones and phases involved like key launch dates, the pre-marketing, the post-production, approvals, the actual execution, the prep, the briefing.

Simple Branded Content Calendar

Date	Hero	Hub	Hygiene
Wk 1			
Wk 2			Hygiene 1
Wk 3			
Wk 4			Hygiene 2
Wk 5		Hub 1	
Wk 6			Hygiene 3
Wk 7			
Wk 8			Hygiene 4
Wk 9			
Wk 10		Hub 2	Hygiene 5
Wk 11			
Wk 12	Hero 1		Hygiene 6

	Prep for the idea, execution. For hygiene ideas, this would be pre-approved, pre-shot.
	Actual execution of the idea.
	Post production and pre-marketing of the idea.
	Launch of the idea.

You can put specific dates. But it gives you a broad plan to work from/ with. You can also choose to bring in some more detail linked to a specific project.

Sample Project-led Branded Content Calendar

Period	Phase 1 PRE	Phase 2 PREP	Phase 3 EXECN	Phase 4 LAUNCH	Phase 5 TRACK
Wk 1	Briefing				
Wk 2	Creator lock				
Wk 3	Creative lock	Contract lock			
Wk 4	Budget lock	Timeline lock			
Wk 5		Advance			
Wk 6		Script lock			
Wk 7		Team lock			
Wk 8		Prep	PPM		
Wk 9		Brief PR, Social	Shoot		
Wk 10			Post		
Wk 11			Post		
Wk 12			Ancillary content	Pre-launch buzz	
Wk 13				Launch, Promotion, PR	
Wk 14					Track, report

And you can list out assets to be delivered in each phase...

Pre-launch	Launch	Post-buzz
Teaser Trailer Poster Social media concepts, posts Launch event Press release Media plan if relevant	Primary content [e.g.: Episode, series] Ancillary content [Behind the scenes, memes, influencer activation] PR interviews Appearances	Bonus content Reviews Extensions Episode cutdowns, exclusives for brand Reports, tracks Social media campaign closures

Again, this is just indicative and you can tweak it to suit your specific project. It's important to have a plan so you can screw around with it, and more importantly, have fun with it.

BUDGETING FOR BRANDED CONTENT

In the ancient times of yore, the content creation budget was often a measly fraction of the media budget. We're talking 10 to 20%, folks. It was like trying to squeeze a watermelon into a tiny fruit basket. And there are some who still, gulp, follow this 'wisdom'!

Movies flip this logic entirely on its head. The promotion budget in the movie biz is often 10 to 20% of the production budget. It's a topsy-turvy world where the balance of power shifts. And guess what? Brands like BMW and Red Bull followed suit. They decided to go against the grain and splurge a disproportionate amount on creating content rather than just distributing it. They shattered the old rules of 'working' vs. 'non-working' budgets, and boy, did it pay off! Audiences today, also want to see that spend on screen!

Now, when it comes to ballpark costs for producing different formats of Branded Content, we're venturing into a minefield of variables. Scale, complexity, talent, objectives – you name it, it impacts the budget. For instance, a song can be half-decently produced for anywhere between INR 10,000 to INR 1 crore [US$ 120 to US$ 1.2 million]. Yeah, it's quite a range, I know. So, attempting to share a ballpark may be a bit of a waste.

But here's the thing: expensive doesn't always equal better. Some inexpensive content pieces have made a massive brand impact. It's like finding a diamond in a pile of [old, smelly] socks. However, bigger budgets can give you a shot at snagging experienced talent, improving production values, and maybe even roping in some familiar faces that boost discoverability. Plus, they can help you build a strong distribution pipe.

Elements to plan for in a Branded Content budget

1. **Ideation, writing:** You gotta invest in developing those killer ideas. It's like the R&D cost of creating a new product. You need

something to work with. If you don't have an ongoing agency or creative team on retainer, you may need to spend on idea development with some freelancers. In fact, that way you may have more options to play with and the ability to bring in the right expertise or skills vs. the same minds who may not be equipped for new formats. Consider exploring multiple ideas before settling on the final one.

2. **Production:** This covers the actual execution of the idea. Costs depend on a ton of factors like the scale, complexity. You can work backward from your budget or forward from the idea, if it really blows your mind. It includes prepping, shooting, post-production, the team involved.

3. **Talent:** The cost of crew and talent is usually part of the budget. But sometimes, you might have some heavy-hitters involved – celebrity talent or special experts with their entourage of hair, make-up, styling, spot boy, driver, dietary demands, conveyance, travel, stay, per diems, terry towels, teddy bears and more. Build that into your budget and make sure the deliverables in return for that fee are clearly outlined including shoot hours, social media shout-outs, PR support and more. It's always good to get someone who is doing it for more than just the money. He/ she/ they are also excited about the brand, the idea and more.

4. **Distribution:** Where you put your Branded Content is as critical as what your content is. Like choosing the perfect stage for your performance. Most media agencies still haven't figured out what to do with communication beyond the traditional 30 seconder. At times, the creative idea will decide where it should

be placed. Traditional TV and digital are just the tip of the iceberg. Think outside the box. A lot of great ideas have got lost buried under the debris of junk on YouTube or a brand's own social media handle. So, plan out, where should it be hosted: Your own platform? An influencer's page/ handle? Released in a multiplex theatre? Premiered at film festival? Performed on the streets? Or in a stadium? Published on an OTT platform? Or a TV channel?

Partnering with existing platforms might require a 'carriage' or 'hosting' fee which can often be off-set against some value like impressions, views, reach, inventory, social media call-outs, promotions committed.

5. **Promotion:** Content is as crowded as a local fast train during rush hour. Even the hottest Branded Content needs a little push to be discovered. The most anticipated films featuring the biggest superstars bet heavy media dollars to make sure they're seen by as many audiences as possible on opening weekend.

6. **Track and Review:** It's worth the investment and it won't break the bank. You might want to set aside a small sum to track and evaluate the performance of your Branded Content. Think of it like taking your shiny new car for a spin and checking under the hood. You want to know how it's performing, right?

   You can go for some focused research or a brand track to get juicy insights on recall, association, key messages, and impact. It's like having a secret weapon to course-correct your current and future campaigns. And the best part? It won't cost you an arm and a leg.

No matter what the content creation ratio is to your marketing budget, one thing's for sure: you *need* to spend on Branded Content. And the need to carve out a budget for it. You can start small, partner up with existing content properties, create some smaller hygiene pieces and gradually build up your experience and expertise. But start.

There's no magic number. But carve out at least a part of your ad budget to begin somewhere and let it rip. Remember, if you multiply anything by zero, it turns into... you guessed it, zero. So, take a leap of faith and see what awaits you on the other side. After all, nothing ventured, nothing gained.

CASE STUDY:
MERE DAD KI MARUTI

Let's dive into something that's probably the first of its kind in India and preceded the Lego Movie by 1 year. Considered a benchmark in Branded Content, Marketing in the Indian Cinema and Automobile Industry, but no one's been able to pull off another one so far. Buckle up!

Background: Maruti Suzuki, launching India's 1st compact SUV

India's leading auto manufacturer, Maruti Suzuki was about to launch their disruptive beast, the Ertiga – a compact SUV backed by their signature service, support and more that would make heads turn.

The Challenge: Make Me Cool!

The mother brand stood for value-for-money and in a very competitive auto market which was seeing a spate of launches [2012-13], Maruti needed to get young, get cool and get the attention of the young, hip crowd. Challenge accepted!

The Plan: Hijack a Bollywood Feature Film

Internationally, there had been a lot of films themed around cars, but India was missing out. Barring a 'Chalti Ka Naam Gaadi', 'Taarzan the Wonder Car'. No Herbie, no Bumblebee. And while placements of cars may have happened, nothing at scale that created impact. There entered this incredible opportunity of a full-fledged Bollywood feature film!

Yash Raj Films, Mere Dad ki Maruti

The youth films division of one of India's leading film studios, Yash Raj Films, Y-Films, was developing a feature around a lost car. Originally titled Mere Dad ki Car, the opportunity for placement was seamless. There were other contenders but Maruti outbid them all and also presented the best thematic fit given how the brand has almost been generic to the category of first/ small cars. Both a pro and a con.

The Placement & Integrations

The film told the story about a boy who sneaks out his stingy dad's fancy new Maruti Suzuki Ertiga to impress the college hottie. And then loses the car. The car is meant to be a gift for his sister who's about to get married in 4 days which ups the personal stakes and places a ticking time-bomb. Along the way he encounters strange characters galore; from a gang of car thieves, a don, a car rental run by geriatric jatts, an enthusiastic salesman, cuckoo relatives and more. The Ertiga seamlessly made its way into multiple scenes, songs, dialogues, dramatic plot points. And, of course, the title besides the theme and core fabric of the film itself. Without for a moment feeling like it's a long advertisement given how smartly it was done. For most marketers, consumers, it was a revelation that the film was funded by Maruti.

The fun and loveable family in the film were hardcore Maruti loyalists, establishing a strong emotional connect. The Ertiga was placed as the object of desire for the young leads making it aspirational and cool. With a soundtrack featuring the biggest names in music from Honey Singh and Mika to Panjabi MC and Diljit Dosanjh. The songs showcased the car in lyrics and videos. A hilarious scene at the showroom with a test drive brought in all the key features so seamlessly that it even surprised the makers! And a shocker of a climax where multiple Marutis make an entry, made it extremely memorable.

The Reach: 100 million+ eyeballs and counting!

The film became a sensation, reaching over 100 million eyeballs. Remember, this was in 2013, before streaming platforms and Jio took over the world, so a million viewers were no joke. The film opened in 45+ cities, which covered all of the Ertiga's priority markets. After a successful theatrical run, it premiered with multiple repeats across Sony Entertainment TV, Sab TV, SET Max besides DTH, in-flight, digital, in-cruise, PPV adding massive reach. The 360-degree marketing campaign delivered over 24,000 TV spots. The songs ran on 20+ music channels, in Ganpati festival celebrations, award shows and through integrations across TV, youth channels, radio, events, digital. PR continued as part of the build-up to the release. Other brands hopped on the bandwagon, promoting the film, and in turn, the car. Red Bull with a special song/video by Nucleya; P&G's car freshener 'AmbiPur' with TV Promos, 'Integriti' apparel with promotions on ground, at stores and on TV. Radio Mirchi, a leading FM station, flipped their traffic updates with the title song as its sting. Social media exploded with dad-son memes, gifs. Car loan companies were using the film's title to sell their policies!

Maruti also didn't pull its punches. They tapped into their massive service and retail network, creating a buzz among customers. Welcome-kits came with CDs [yeah, we still had those back then], ticket giveaways as sales incentives, consumer contests, airtime on TV, cricket matches and more.

View, Reviews and Love

The earned media on the film was enormous. There was media coverage across dailies nationally, with 100% carriage of the brand name – talking about cast performances, the humor, the songs, and the car – clocking upwards of INR 100 million+ in value. The movie made its way into every year end list of Top 10 films to watch.

★★★★
KOMAL NAHTA
What an entertainer!

★★★
NDTV
Mere Dad ki Maruti a winner!

★★★★½
DOORDARSHAN
Young, vibrant, full punju power!

★★★½
TARAN ADARSH
Mazedaar, Masaledaar, full-on entertainer!

★★★
RAJEEV MASAND
Light & easy!

★★★
TIMES OF INDIA
Take dad along in his gaddi!

★★★
MUMBAI MIRROR
Zooms out in top gear!

★★★½
MID-DAY
Definitely a fun ride!

★★★
BOOKMYSHOW
A complete battery-charge!

★★★½
RJ JEETURAJ
Radio Mirchi, Super hilarious family entertainment!

★★★½
RAJA SEN
Rediff.com, Give it a whirl!

★★★½
PLANET BOLLYWOOD
Can't miss this 'car-nama'!

★★★½
BOX OFFICE CAPSULE
Perfect recipe for teenagers!

★★★½
IN.COM
A ride we recommend!

★★★
ENTERTAINMENT OF INDIA
What an entertainer!

★★★
KOIMOI.COM
Give your popcorn a miss, enjoy this mad comic caper!

★★★
GLAMSHAM
More power to youth!

★★★
BOLLYWOOD LIFE
Makes you smile and giggle!

★★★
SANTA BANTA
Vroom joy ride!

★★★½
DESI MARTINI
A zippy fun ride!

Rumors of a sequel further fuelled stories. The coverage continued for weeks pre and post release. And later when the marketing tie-in was revealed, the business media/pink papers went into overdrive covering the one-of-a-kind innovation.

A year into the release, the CEO of Infosys, one of India's largest corporates, Vishal Sikka was featured on the front page of India's #1 Business Daily, The Economic Times, talking about how his favorite film that he'd watched 3 to 4 times with his son was Mere Dad ki Maruti.

Vishal Sikka, CEO, Infosys

The Economic Times, August 1st 2014 on MDKM

Business Impact: 30% spike in test drives!

The most powerful barometer in the auto business for evaluating marketing campaigns, is test drives. Whether it converted to footfalls in showrooms? Mere Dad ki Maruti drove up test drives for the Ertiga by 30%, outstripping even Maruti's own expectations. This could directly be attributed to the film as there was no other thematic advertising running around the promotional and release window of the feature film. There were huge lifts in likability for the Ertiga, and in spontaneous recall for 3 of the key features of the car that Maruti wanted to plug as differentiators. Showrooms were buzzing with excitement, and every media agency was scratching its head, trying to figure how to replicate this for their clients. Those 30-second TV commercials felt so last season. The Maruti Suzuki Ertiga became one of the most talked about car launches in the industry for a long time.

CASE STUDY: RANVEER CHING

You know, jingles, song & dance routines and celebrities endorsing products have been around longer than your grandma's secret recipe. But let me tell you, what went down with Ching's Secret was a brand-building, branded content extravaganza like you've never seen before in the packaged foods category. It was so big; it made the big boys squirm in their fancy corporate chairs.

Background: Taking on the Giants!

Capital Foods had a brand called Ching's Secret offering Indian Chinese Masalas, Soups, Sauces, and Noodles. Now, they were up against Nestle's Maggi, the undisputed heavyweight champ of the category with a 3-decade lead, along with other giants like ITC's Yippee and Unilever's Knorr. Ching's was just a local player with big dreams of going national.

The Challenge: Look at Me, Ma!

Ching's had one major obstacle to overcome – nobody knew they existed! The category's communication was stuck in a time warp, with the tropes of hungry kids and moms whipping up a meal in [2] minutes. We had to break free from those cliches and stand out from the big boys' extravagant spends.

The Plan: Kill Mom!

Cuisine changes every 5 kilometres in India, but there's one thing that unites it – the love for movies and Indian Chinese. So, we decided to blow up the category templates, leave mom behind, and forget about those mundane 30-second TV commercials. We weren't interested in having the celebrity hold the product either. No, no, no! We needed someone with a touch of craziness and charisma, and that's where the maverick, Ranveer Singh, entered the scene.

Enter Mr. Ranveer Singh & Team

This was back in 2014, so Ranveer had delivered no major hits after his smashing debut. The only brand he endorsed at the time was Durex condoms, a category, most celebrities stayed away from endorsing, which gives you an idea of his wild side. We assembled an A-list Bollywood crew that created the smokescreen that there was actually a new Ranveer movie in the pipeline. Shaad Ali as director, Gulzar saab for lyrics, Shankar-Ehsaan-Loy for music, Ganesh Acharya for choreography, and Yash Raj Films to distribute the film and music. We embedded the brand so seamlessly into the content that the lines between brand, entertainment AND talent completely blurred.

Singh is Ching

A thumping, chart-busting song and music video featuring a colorful character called 'Ranveer Ching'. The brand name was part of the catchy hook line and chorus. The video was young, energetic, and hotter than a freshly cooked samosa.

We treated it like a movie, dropping teasers, posters, trailers, and song promos populating the digital eco-system of telecom companies, music on web. Ranveer even changed his social media handle to Ranveer Ching!

Trade on Fire!

Sales teams were buzzing, retail outlets were drooling with anticipation. The campaign set audio streams on fire with downloads, high rotations, spins across 17+ music channels, radio stations. We generated PR worth almost 100 million rupees. People couldn't stop talking about it!

Quotes Priya Chanda, GroupM Director on Knorr, *"#MyNameIsRanveerChing is truly the best marketing campaign of the year!"* Manita Panwani, GM Marketing, McDonald's, *"Incredible campaign, can it be replicated for McD's, how the hell was it done?"* Ameya Sule, Business Director, GroupM ESP, *"Ching's is a total clutter-breaker, content integration done so smartly vs. the classic*

30-sec TVC." Amar Thomas, CMO, Blackberry, *"Fantastic innovation, put Ching's on the map... when does the movie come out?"*

Business Impact

From 70,000 stores in August 2014, the distribution reach of Ching's skyrocketed 4x to a mind-boggling 280,000 stores by December 2015. Ching's soup became #1 in Maharashtra and Gujarat. And most importantly, gained MASSIVE SHARE OF MIND.

Upping the Game: Movie follows the Music

We were riding high on the wave of success, but it was time to take things to the next level. We wanted to own a cuisine block. 'Desi Chinese'. Go wider nationally and dig deeper into the south. And squeeze the value out of this ridiculously successful campaign. So, we decided to produce a BLOCKBUSTER mini-movie. And who better to bring this bad boy to life than the one and only, Michael Masala Bay of Bollywood: Rohit Shetty. We roped in popular southern stars, Tamannah Bhatia and Pradeep to add the south connect.

Ranveer Ching Returns

With Rohit on board, we cooked up a dystopian world where hunger reigned supreme, and the only saviour was our Desi Chinese Warrior, Ranveer Ching. Think Mad Max meets Bollywood on steroids! We had cars flying, things blowing up, catchy one-liners that hit harder than a punch to the gut, and, of course, some killer song and dance numbers... the original track remixed by a hotshot DJ. The film premiered at a single screen for select media, trade and consumers. And boy, did jaws drop! We're talking 11 million+ views organically [again, this was back in 2016 when high-speed internet was still a luxury in India]. The ancillary content also raked up 5 million+ views. The campaign front-paged on dailies, entertainment, and business media. Movie critics like Taran Adarsh, Komal Nahta, Anupama Chopra, Rajeev Masand were reviewing a TVC! Yeah, a TVC, folks!

Continued Business Impact

We had everyone from Unilever bigwigs to the legendary Amitabh Bachchan [who used to endorse Maggi] raving about our campaign on social media. Sony TV ran promos for the premiere of the ad on their channel. And brace yourselves for the results: a 72% lift in ad recall, 452% jump in brand interest [unprecedented in the category], 1000% lift in search across markets. Massive impact in target markets – especially Tamil Nadu, Karnataka, and Telangana.

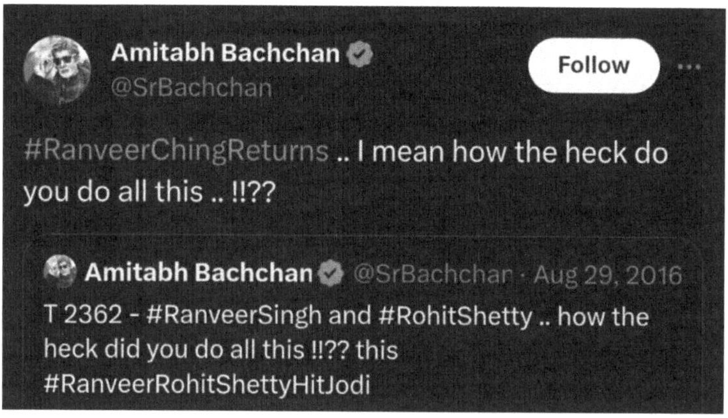

The masala business grew by a staggering 45%. Distributors from small towns in UP, Bihar and Jharkhand were lining up to get their hands on the product. The export orders grew by over 100%. The cherry on top? The topline more than tripled in under three freakin' years.

The campaign is living proof of how betting on the right Branded Content can help a challenger brand take on the biggies. One mouth-watering bowl of Desi Chinese at a time!

CASE STUDY: UNILEVER & 6-PACK BAND

Another mind-blowing first in India and possibly the world. A big ol' legacy brand, Unilever's Brooke Bond Red Label tea stepped up to support a marginalized community, making an impact that went way beyond its business. Here's how India's 1st Transgender Band helped make the world a more welcoming place.

Background: Not everyone's cup of tea

Unilever's Brooke Bond Red Label Tea is a hundred-year-old brand that targets folks from tier 2 and 3, from a lower socio-economic background. It'd been all warm and fuzzy advertising over the years, but let's be real, tea isn't exactly the most exciting thing in the world. It's like, *"Hey, wanna chat about tea?"* cut to crickets chirping.

The Challenge: Build a storm in a teacup

So, Brooke Bond wanted to stir things up, create some serious engagement, and make a splash in the West and North markets. They wanted to show that their tea is more than just a beverage, it's a social lubricant that brings people closer, breaks down social barriers, and gets the conversation flowing. Bring it on!

The Plan: Don't talk about taboos, sing about 'em

This was in 2015, and the LGBTQ movement was gaining momentum. It was all over the place, from President Obama gracing the cover of a gay magazine 'Open', to gay marriages being legalized. Even the Indian Supreme Court recognized the 3rd gender. Caitlyn Jenner, Laverne Cox, Eddie Redmayne in Danish Girl, and Transparent at the Emmies were making waves too. The stage was set.

Now, in India, the trans community, known as the 'hijras', faced massive stigma. They were often pushed into prostitution or left with no choice but to beg for a living. But here's the thing: they were also known for their incredible musicality and performed during festivals, weddings, and even the birth of a child.

India's 1st Transgender Band

We scoured the entire nation to find 6 outrageously talented and beautiful members from the trans community to form the 6-Pack Band. Oh, and why six? Well, it's a play on 'chhakka', which is a term that can be used derogatorily to refer to the community. But it also means a sixer in Cricket, like hitting it out of the park. Plus, who doesn't want a killer six-pack, right?

Superstar Hrithik Roshan with the 6-Pack Band

We created six songs and six music videos, each one smashing different myths and misconceptions. And to add some Bollywood glitz and glam, we teamed up with big names like Anushka Sharma, Sonu Nigam, Hrithik Roshan, Shahrukh Khan, Arjun Kapoor, and more. Folks known for championing inclusion, and they brought with them their large fanbases.

Pharrell Williams would be 'Happy'

We kicked things off with a unique cover of Pharrell's hit, 'Happy'. A conscious choice to give it global relevance. And then brought in Hindi, Marathi for resonance in the West and North markets.

'Happy' was followed up with a song that told the real-life story of one of the band members, capturing their journey from being ostracised to eventually being accepted. It borrowed an iconic couplet from a holy book, reminding everyone that we're all children of the same God.

The lyrics cleverly emphasized how tea leaves don't give a damn about the color, race, religion, or gender of the person drinking it. And one of the songs was actually composed using tea cups, spoons, Brooke Bond Red Label packs as a style of Stomp Music. Talk about tea-infused tunes! The brand integrations were seamless and the band was launched as the hottest new music act on the scene.

6-Pack hits a six!

The premiere of their first song hit the fastest 1 million in under 24 hours. That's right, an independent music act achieving something unheard of at the time. It caught the attention of consumers and influencers alike, generating massive social buzz, millions of views, and non-stop chatter. We're talking over 150 million bucks worth of earned media, airplay across music channels, and radio stations. The band even performed at one of the most prestigious Music Awards [Radio Mirchi] in the country, and they got invited to the hottest late night talk shows, like the Kapil Sharma show [think India's Kimmel/ Fallon]. They received love from across the globe, with Eliot Page [Ellen Page then] flying all the way to India to feature the band in Vice's 'Gaycation'.

6 Pack Band backstage with Shahrukh Khan

Let's not forget the accolades! The 6-Pack Band brought home India's 1st Cannes Grand Prix Glass Lion, and we had powerhouses like Sheryl Sandberg and Geena Davis talking about it. They were among the Top 5 Honorees at the 2016 Webby's worldwide, and racked up close to 40+ shiny metals across various creative and effectiveness awards. Oh, and just to casually drop it, yours truly made it to the 2016 AdAge Global Top 50 Creative List alongside the likes of JJ Abrams, David Fincher, Ted Sarandos, Banksy and Pharrell Williams!

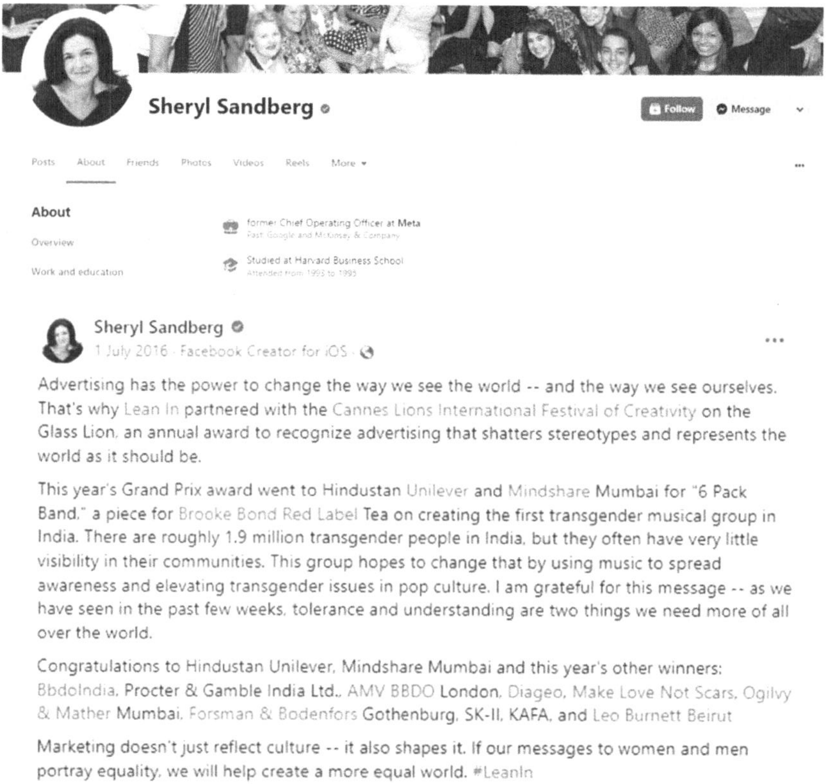

Sheryl Sandberg

Follow Message

Posts About Friends Photos Videos Reels More

About

Overview

Work and education

former Chief Operating Officer at Meta

Studied at Harvard Business School

Sheryl Sandberg

1 July 2016 · Facebook Creator for iOS

Advertising has the power to change the way we see the world -- and the way we see ourselves. That's why Lean In partnered with the Cannes Lions International Festival of Creativity on the Glass Lion, an annual award to recognize advertising that shatters stereotypes and represents the world as it should be.

This year's Grand Prix award went to Hindustan Unilever and Mindshare Mumbai for "6 Pack Band," a piece for Brooke Bond Red Label Tea on creating the first transgender musical group in India. There are roughly 1.9 million transgender people in India, but they often have very little visibility in their communities. This group hopes to change that by using music to spread awareness and elevating transgender issues in pop culture. I am grateful for this message -- as we have seen in the past few weeks, tolerance and understanding are two things we need more of all over the world.

Congratulations to Hindustan Unilever, Mindshare Mumbai and this year's other winners: BbdoIndia, Procter & Gamble India Ltd., AMV BBDO London, Diageo, Make Love Not Scars, Ogilvy & Mather Mumbai, Forsman & Bodenfors Gothenburg, SK-II, KAFA, and Leo Burnett Beirut

Marketing doesn't just reflect culture -- it also shapes it. If our messages to women and men portray equality, we will help create a more equal world. #LeanIn

Brand & Business Impact: Outsold category by 1.3x

This campaign wasn't just about making noise; it made a real impact. A whopping 84% of viewers associated the content with the brand. 64% consumers perceived the brand made the world a more welcoming place after experiencing this campaign. Brand penetration shot up by over 400 basis points, and Brooke Bond Red Label Tea grew 1.3 times as compared to the packaged tea category. That's how you stir things up!

And Beyond

But the most powerful result was when one of the band members received a call from her father after 11 long years. Her own family had disowned her when she embraced her true identity, her sexual orientation, and her preferences. From being Kamlesh to Komal. No award, no revenue, no words can ever match up to the impact of that moment. Because that's when content goes beyond just delivering impact. It delivers meaning.

So, raise your teacups to the 6-Pack Band, a group of extraordinary individuals who rocked the world and spread love, acceptance, and a whole lot of musical magic. Cheers to making the world a better place, one soulful sip and song at a time!

MEASURING IMPACT OF BRANDED CONTENT

Measuring Branded Content may feel like trying to solve a Rubik's Cube blindfolded. It's tricky, but not impossible. Unlike traditional advertising, Branded Content aims for a deeper emotional connection with the audience, you can't rely on standard metrics like impressions and click-through rates. You need to dig deeper to capture the true impact and engagement with your content.

Some metrics to help you to evaluate their effectiveness

1. **Reach & Views:** How far has your content travelled? Look at the number of views and exposure across various platforms and channels. It's like measuring the wingspan of a bald eagle – it gives you a basic idea of the content's reach.

2. **Engagement & Interaction:** Content consumption is no longer passive. People want to talk about it, find out more, diss it, celebrate it, make it their own. The worst thing that can happen to it, is being ignored. Measure engagement through likes, shares, comments, audience versions, participation and other interactions. Even if the primary medium where it's hosted is non-interactive, eventually the spill on to social and more is what can give you a fair indication of its performance. It's like determining how many people joined the conga line at a party – the higher the engagement, the greater the impact.

3. **Completion Rates:** Is your content holding the audience's attention? Look at the percentage of people who start and finish watching, reading, or experiencing the entire piece. Are they putting it away after the first bite, half-way through, licking the plate clean and/ or going back for second helpings? A great indicator of how delicious your dish is.

4. **Brand Mentions & Sentiment:** Are people chatting about your brand in relation to your Branded Content? It's like eavesdropping on what your audience thinks about your creation – unlike those focus groups with 'chivda' eating aunties where people try and test creative ideas [worst idea ever!]. Monitor social media platforms and online

conversations to gauge brand mentions and sentiment. Are they singing your praises or giving you the stink-eye? It's like listening in on a coffee shop conversation – sentiment reveals how your content shakes and shapes brand perception. These are like free focus groups!

5. **Virality & Shareability:** Is your content spreading like wildfire or collecting dust? Track shares, retweets, reposts, memes, GIFs and more to measure its viral potential. It's like determining if your content is a contagious yawn or a catchy earworm – virality indicates resonance and whether it has the potential to reach a wider audience.

6. **Media Coverage & PR:** Keep an eye on press mentions, articles, interviews, reviews, and features about your content. Besides brand mentions, earned media value, quality of the coverage in terms of pictures, headlines, captions, position, size. This will help gauge the level of interest and buzz created by your campaign, "Look Ma, I'm on TV!"

7. **Brand Recall & Association:** Do people remember your brand and connect it with the content? Conduct surveys and studies to assess brand recall and association. It could be a simple Google Survey or detailed Brand Tracks. It's like quizzing a goldfish on its memory skills – these metrics will provide insights into the effectiveness in leaving a lasting brand impression.

8. **Specific Objectives:** Evaluate the campaign against the specific goals set, be it subscriber count, downloads, footfalls to store, brand lift, likeability, marketing leads, other. It's like ticking off

items on your shopping list – QR codes, affiliate links, coupon codes, contest entry/ participation can help track progress.

9. **Awards & Recognition:** I'm not a huge fan of this, but industry awards and recognition can indicate how well your content is received by peers and the wider industry. "I'd like to thank God, my mom, my dog Happy Patil, my..."

10. **Business Impact:** Ultimately, the bottom-line matters. Analyse how your Branded Content influences consumer behaviour and purchasing decisions and in turn sales, revenue, market share, customer acquisition. Business impact measures the tangible business outcomes of your campaign.

Sample Branded Content goals and associated metrics

Note, that these are the more here & now kind of objectives vs. the broader ones of building trust, loyalty, connection, positive associations, perception shifts that happen over a medium to longer term with consumers.

Goals	Possible Metrics
Brand awareness	Traffic to website, social handles Page/ Video views Downloads Social chatter Referral links
Engagement	Blog comments Likes, shares, tweets, forwards
Lead generation	Form completions, downloads Email subscriptions

	Blog subscriptions Conversion rate
Sales	Online sales Offline sales
Customer retention/ loyalty	Percentage of content consumed by existing customers Retention/ renewal rates

Now, depending on the format of Branded Content, the Key Performance Indicators can be further drilled down. These overlap with more traditional media evaluation tools but are a good starting point.

KPIs for Different Formats of Branded Content

Format	KPI
Video content	Views Unique viewers Average view duration Subscribers Impressions Click-through rates YouTube CTA click-throughs Shares Comments Traffic sources Reviews, ratings
Podcasts, audio	Streams Subscribers Backlinks Downloads Social shares Reviews, ratings

Social media	Followers, fans Conversation rate Landing page conversion rate Post reach Sentiment
Blogs, articles, short/ long-form written content	Traffic to site, social pages Unique visitors New vs. returning visitors Time spent on site Average time on page Bounce rate Exit rate Page views Page views per visit Traffic sources Geographic trends Mobile vs. desktop visitors Profile of visitors

Remember, the choice of metrics depends on your campaign objectives and goals. Align your measurement approach with the specific outcomes you aim to achieve through your Branded Content. And sometimes, the real measure of success is the joy you bring to people's lives – just like a perfectly cooked batch of unicorn-shaped pancakes.

EXPERT SPEAK | CREATOR PERSPECTIVE: TANMAY BHAT

Tanmay is a writer, producer, director, stand-up comic, curator, ad man, tech-entrepreneur, and more rolled into one. Always someone who's pushed the envelope, often tearing it [I mean, who uses envelopes and letters to deliver messages anymore anyway?!], to shape humor and pop culture in our country. The stellar work he and his team have done across brands, be it Cred, Lenskart, Shark Tank, Bold Care and more screams out because it is beyond just clever, funny content. *It is rooted in great consumer insight; it has a unique tone that is on brand and it entertains. It straddles a space that goes beyond advertising, gives ad agencies sleepless nights and clients hard-ons. Here, he shares some of his process in cooking up what he does.*

AP: Alright, spit it out! How do you manage to integrate brands into your content without losing your authenticity? It's like trying to rock a superhero suit while staying true to your secret identity. Any tips and tricks up your creative sleeves?

Tanmay: There isn't any special trick. The fundamental insight is people go about their daily lives and they consume things that are inherently interesting to them. A brand is never at the centre of anybody's lives. Nobody actively wants to watch an ad. So, you serve them content – the thing they want to consume. Be it a brand integration in a YouTube video – or an actual TVC. This, of course, sounds clichéd, but it truly is the only thing that works.

A good litmus test for anybody working in branded content is: does the team enjoy the process of writing it or producing it. If the writers are laughing, if the people on set are laughing, it is likely enjoyable for the viewer to watch.

AP: We all love a good collaboration, especially when it elevates the storytelling experience. Give us the lowdown on some of your successful Branded Content projects. How did they make your audience scream with delight? Did you have them at "product placement"?

Tanmay: I think some of the most popular ads I've written are the Cred advertisements. I'd never written a television commercial before. I didn't know how to write one. So, I just followed what I would usually do: What is fun for me to watch?

I'd heard horror stories about interfering clients, bloated bureaucratic structures within agencies that would often result in a compromised creative. But I experienced none of that.

We were a lean team of 4 writers – Kunal and Trupti from Cred's end and Ayappa the director. And that's it. Kunal had given us full freedom to pursue what we wanted. And so, the onus was on the creative team to deliver. So, for the first time - everybody from the writers, to the makers of the ad – felt like they were the client. Which is usually not how the advertising process works – there's usually a client who's looking to make sure that the brand is represented well. There is the agency and the production company that wants to win creatively and add to their showreel. But we felt none of that. It felt like one team.

Regarding the creative: We were targeting credit card holders – so often that meant somebody who's in their 30's and 40's. Affluent and from modern India. So, we chose celebrities who would be appealing to this cohort. And we made creatives that we would enjoy watching with them. And the rest is history.

AP: So, when you're scouting for brand partnerships, what criteria do you use? How do you make sure it's a match made in marketing heaven? And most importantly, how do you prevent any awkward moments if your brand's a rogue vigilante and theirs' a mild-mannered reporter?

Tanmay: There's no easy way of figuring if the brand and you are a right fit until you take a journey together, unfortunately. I think a call where everybody understands that we have to be engaging for as long as possible – is the easiest way. And, of course, there should be one key decision maker that drives the creative project. Creativity is not a democracy. It is a dictatorship.

AP: Behind every great Branded Content project, there's a collaborative process that's messier than Deadpool's sense of humor. Maintaining the integrity of your content while integrating a brand's messaging sounds trickier than defying gravity. How do you keep it real? How do you make sure the brand integration doesn't feel forced, like an ill-fitting superhero cape?

Tanmay: It's not as tricky as people make it out to be. No matter what you're trying to sell – there is always an interesting way to sell it. One key insight – and I don't know if this fits in this question is – it always helps if the buyer has a sense of taste. I've noticed that companies where the key decision makers have some sort of an artistic pursuit themselves – buy the best ideas. If your brand manager is a musician, or a poet, or a comedian or if they have any artistic pursuit – they know what pleases an audience. Hence, they're able to visualize the end product a lot better. Often, I tell founders to hire folks with a creative bent to be in the company. It elevates the overall taste of the company.

AP: The audience is the ultimate judge of our entertainment choices. How do you gauge their response to your Branded Content projects? Are there secret metrics or feedback channels you rely on? Or do you just hang out on social media, wearing a disguise, to eavesdrop on their conversations?

Tanmay: Just watch your own habits on social media. What attracts you? What do you watch? <u>You'll come to the conclusion that the opposite of love isn't hate. It is being ignored</u>. If you manage to get attention, you have won.

AP: Alright, creator-to-creator advice time! Imagine you're mentoring a fresh-faced creator eager to dip their toes into the Branded Content pool. What pearls of wisdom would you drop on them? What should they consider before jumping into bed, metaphorically speaking, with a brand?

Tanmay: Remember that you're in the branded content business to make money. And somebody else is spending that money. And complaining about how they're spending their money not buying your idea is futile. We all love to complain when it's somebody else's money at stake. But we would understand when we make that spend ourselves. I have a lot of empathy for founders and companies. It's not easy to decide to try do something risky. Especially when you've built a company for years with a lot of love.

AP: Time for some crystal ball gazing! What future trends do you see shaping the world of Branded Content? How do you think the relationship between creators and brands will evolve in the coming years? Will we finally see a team-up to rival the Avengers?

Tanmay: Attention is the new oil. If you master how to build and to sell – you can be king. Great creators master how to sell. Now, it's time for them to build :)

EXPERT SPEAK | BRAND/ CLIENT PERSPECTIVE: AJAY GUPTA

Ajay Gupta, Managing Director, Capital Foods, is a foodie trapped in a marketing, sales and distribution head's body. 35+ years of a range of experiences across Advertising, Marketing and Distribution eventually led him to set up one of the fastest growing brands in the Food Processing Industry that includes Ching's Desi Chinese, Smith & Jones. Innovation, disruption and risk-taking always drives everything he's done across products, packaging, pricing, and of course, marketing. Ajay opens up about what drives him to punt on Branded Content.

AP: Alright, brand superhero, what made you say, "Let's try Branded Content!" Was it a divine vision from the marketing gods? And how has this genius move helped you forge a special connection with your audience? Did you send them all a secret handshake?

Ajay: We believe that there are 3 religions in India that reach the masses. The 3 Cs really – Cricket, Cinema and Chinese that's Desi. So, combining Desi Chinese with Cinema, or rather, Bollywood, for us was the right way of reaching the hinterland of the country. For me, that is really not 'divine', it's common sense!

AP: Show me the money! I mean, show me some epic examples of your Branded Content campaigns. How did they skyrocket your brand's story and engage those hard-to-impress consumers? Did you have them at "product placement"? Or did you secretly hire a brainwashing squad?

Ajay: We don't think of it as 'product placement'. We work on 'product integration'. And there is a big difference between product placement in entertainment when compared to integration. What we have done each time is integrated our brand into the storytelling itself. The best example here is how we integrated Ching's Schezwan Chutney into Rohit Shetty's movie, 'Golmaal'. All the characters, from Gopu, Lucky, Laxman 1, Laxman 2, Madhav are shown fighting over the chutney at a meal. It connects with the consumers because it's part of the story and therefore makes our product larger than life – which works from an aspirational perspective for Indian consumers.

AP: Integrating a brand into entertainment content can be like trying to fit into a spandex suit two sizes too small. What obstacles did you face on this daring adventure, and how did you emerge victorious? Come on, share those valuable lessons like a good secret agent.

Ajay: Bollywood is unique because it is the only film genre in the world which does storytelling through songs and musicals. So that's really what we did.

It was about understanding the essence of Bollywood that has entertained Indians for more than the last 100 years. Then you take this essence and integrate entertainment with the brand. This manifested in our branded music video, 'My name is Ranveer Ching'.

Most of the times people try and do a fit between entertainment and brand – and it's a force-fit – without understanding the essence of what makes the Indian consumer tick. Why we succeed and many others don't is because of our understanding that the essence of Bollywood is musicals. We've been humming songs forever. Even our storytelling of the epics is often sung – be it the Ramayan or the Mahabharat. And that's what we did with 'My Name is Ranveer Ching' – we turned the brand story into a musical production.

Our brand Ching's is exciting, different and quirky. So, our branded content has to be equally quirky and hatke. That's how we make the fit happen.

<u>There are no obstacles! Obstacles are in your head</u>! When we first considered a branded music video internally, we looked at each other, laughed and said, *"Kar daalte hain!"* Kaunsa obstacle tha issmein? None!

AP: Balancing brand promotion and authentic entertainment is like walking a tightrope while juggling chainsaws. How did you manage to keep it real and engaging for your audience? Any

secret ninja moves you'd like to share? Do you have a cape that doubles as a parachute?

Ajay: It's all about how you maintain the balance between the brand and the form of entertainment. If it is storytelling, Bollywood-style, you choose what fits with what you want to communicate. To raise brand saliency, we had a music video, 'My name is Ranveer Ching'. To launch the concept of 'Ching's Desi Chinese' we created a mini blockbuster movie where, in a dystopian world people are dying of hunger and the hero, Ranveer Ching, saves them with Desi Chinese. In a superhero genre, we had Captain Ranveer Ching who consumes Ching's Schezwan Chutney, takes off like a rocket and saves the planet from a meteor. The quirkiness of these stories is pure Bollywood. The executional style is Bollywood entertainment – which is what our consumers understand – and the brand story is told within that.

When consumers look at entertainment, they only want to get entertained. And that becomes the foremost job – to entertain. How you fit the brand in is what is what you work upon then and not the reverse of that. It's not about thinking of a problem-solution situation and then trying to force-fit it into some form of entertainment. It should start with the form of entertainment first and then fit the brand story within it. Typically, everybody looks at a problem-solution idea and then says, "Oh let's think of a quirky execution idea." We first think about the entertainment as an idea, then ask "Can we fit our brand in it?" and then match the brand story to the entertainment genre. Everybody first says, *"Train aa gayi. Abhi engine fit kaise karoon?"*, instead of saying, *"Engine yeh hai, aur ab yeh train fit ho hi jayegi uske saath!"*

AP: Choosing the perfect creator or entertainment platform for your brand integration requires the precision of an Olympic archer. What factors do you consider when making this critical decision? Tell us about the wild world of collaboration between your brand and content creators. How do you ensure that both parties are in sync with the creative vision and objectives? Do you send them matching friendship bracelets?

Ajay: To the producer or director of our advertising it's never about just working with a brand ambassador. Our chosen hero is a brand fit – a personification of the brand. It's not about taking any celebrity and saying OK. You cannot take a serious actor and ask him to say, *"Buy Ching's!"* – it doesn't fit. Like Ashiish says, *"Kaale ghaney lambay baal wala brief."* It's about thinking whether this individual and his persona are similar to the brand's.

Even when it comes to the director, we think whether the director has a persona that fits the brand persona. Because when this happens, the storytelling that comes out automatically carries the brand story with it, which otherwise would not happen. So, all personalities have to match. So, for a particular story where we had a mom and kids setting required with quirky, warm humor, we went to a director like Maneesh Sharma – known for his flavoursome work with Band Baaja Baaraat, Shuddh Desi Romance, Dum Lagaa ke Haisha; for another story where we needed high drama, over the top action, we went with Rohit Shetty for masaaledar, blockbuster storytelling. If we had flipped the two it would have been a disaster!

So, the storytelling has to be seamless – from the protagonist to the person who's directing. Putting the whole thing together has to be seamless as well. They all need to have the same style, and the same mindset.

Now the question is how do you ensure that both parties are in sync with the brand's creative vision and objectives? When we brief directors, we tell them about the company, how we arrived there and bring them up to date on where we are and what is it that we are looking at. The script is not written by us and just given to them. There is an open discussion about the marketing challenges, objectives of the brand – and the script actually comes from there – and not going the top-down way saying, *"Here's my script. Now you produce it!"*

So, when you go in there with such directors, using this process, then you're not expecting to come out with a typical, problem-solution kind of production. Because the director is now living with the story of the brand. He is into it. He is not just doing this as a job. He is actually delivering his soul, his mind, his persona which comes through in the film. You're making them feel like part of the team and telling them that we're on the same side. So, they also start thinking from the brand's point of view.

That is when it's worked for us – when you brief them as if they are they all part of the marketing team and not mere executors, when we sit and talk to them as partners and not just executors of a brief.

AP: Time to get all scientific on me! How do you measure the success and impact of your Branded Content endeavours? What metrics and indicators do you use to evaluate if you're conquering the world of brand awareness, customer loyalty, or even world domination? Is there a secret decoder ring involved?

Ajay: When we first started down the road of Branded Content in 2014, our objective was very clear – we wanted a mega leap in our brand saliency for Ching's. Consumer research done in 2013 told us that awareness of the brand Ching's and its products was inconsistent. After the phenomenon of Ranveer Ching, brand saliency shot up like anything. And our 'risk' really paid off.

Since then, our investment in Branded Content, be it with Ranveer Ching, or with other brand integration initiatives has returned dividends in the form of a 25% CAGR year on year – something that is unheard of in the FMCG category. When we measure our sales figures, we have concluded that wherever there are 500 families in the world, there is Ching's available!

AP: We've all had those "oops" moments, even the best of us. Has there ever been a time when your brand's integration into content fell flat like a deflated bouncy castle? How did you bounce back from that epic fail? Did you hire a team of trained clowns to distract the audience?

Ajay: Our 'Oops!' moment happened when we failed miserably with trying out Branded Content for our other brand, Smith & Jones. The director never actually imbibed the brand and acted only like an executor. The storytelling went haywire and we ended up with a pathetic hash job. I believe it is because the director and the celebrity did not become a part of the marketing team and partner us in this venture. They just took an idea and executed it, without bringing themselves into the game. It was just a job that had to be done from their point of view. And this was when we learnt a great lesson: if you can't bring them in as part of our team, it's not going to work. We can only blame ourselves for being unable to bring them onboard as team members. Maybe we also got carried away with the success of Ching's and did not integrate them properly into our team and left it only as pure execution and that's why it fell flat.

Post this debacle, we relooked at the brand Smith & Jones and defined its persona more clearly. We understood its role in our brand portfolio. Rather than saying it was about international or global cuisine, the brand now enables consumers to make aspirational dishes easily. Given this persona, we would need to now re-consider what kind of Branded Content would work for this brand.

AP: The entertainment world is crazier than a David Lynch and David Dhawan crossover. How do you see Branded Content evolving in this ever-changing landscape? Any emerging trends or strategies that make you want to do a happy dance? Are we talking holograms, jetpacks, or interactive brain implants?

Ajay: The concept of 'entertainment' itself has evolved. It has become very personalized – it's, 'Me and My Screen' – be it the television screen with OTT, be it the computer screen, or a phone screen. Social media or OTT – and I consider OTT in a way to be in the same genre as social media. It's very personalized. The choices you make even on OTT are very personalized. Our interpretation of social media is, 'I decide what I want to see, not what you want to show me.' And that's social media today and that's also the independence of choices on OTT. You decide when you want to see it and what you want to see – hence Branded Content has to change as well. You need to seamlessly be part of this entertainment is which is very individualistic.

Today it can't be one kind of entertainment for all. It's become far more difficult now to entertain people. You're seeing blockbuster movies bomb and you're seeing a movie that comes out of nowhere and is a huge success. That's because each one is saying that's MY entertainment. So, it's far tougher, far more challenging also. And yet the opportunity to entertain is so much more.

It's challenging from a perspective of one shoe doesn't fit all anymore and hence you need to keep working on entertaining so many people all the time. But then you have so many actors coming up and there are so many so-called influencers coming in. So, if you know what you want, it becomes easy. And to me the insight here is, 'Me and My Screen'. That is what is important. If you forget this and start doing stupid things or get caught up with trending buzzwords, you're going to fail.

Even our recipe videos are entertaining people! The last recipe we did got 1.5 million views! A recipe video produced for Rupees 4,000 has turned out to be far more entertaining than a lot of heavily produced content! So, the definition of 'entertainment' itself has changed. Today what entertains me is very personal to me.

Entertaining people is challenging. But we at Capital Foods are discovering that there is 'entertainment' in recipes too!

AP: Brand gurus, we need your wisdom! If you had to give advice to fellow brands itching to embark on a Branded Content adventure, what would it be? Any key considerations or tips you'd like to share with those ready to take the leap? Should they wear a cape and learn how to fly?

Ajay: I believe 'mass communication', as we know it, is dead! It's now communication between you and your screen – on your TV, phone, desktop or laptop. It's only about 'Me and My Screen'. So, I need communication or entertainment that is so personalized. And if you don't embark on this journey and understand this, you're going to fail.

EXPERT SPEAK | CREATOR PERSPECTIVE: ASHISH CHANCHLANI

Ashish is a writer, producer, director, and one of the brightest and funniest young digital creators in the business. His sketch-comedy shorts, the characters he's created over the years and even promotional tie-ins with films, series and brands are legendary with cumulative views sitting north of 4.5 billion! Ashish writes, produces his own material and has over a 55 million strong community that laps up everything that he puts out. I had a hard time transcribing his voice notes, given how funny they were. Ashish breaks down his process of partnering with brands and creating solutions that rock and deliver the funnies as well.

AP: So, what's the secret sauce? How do you manage to blend brands into your content without losing your authentic flavor? Any recipes for success you can share?

Ashish: *Sacchi bolu Ashiish Bhai?* Koi aisa secret sauce nahi hai. We feel that when we make any content, the whole country should relate to it. I've shifted to Mumbai now; I've only recently got a house in Bandra but I am originally from Ulhasnagar. One tiny little suburb which is like really far out. So, I've seen, had friends and relatives who are from the 'tier-2' audience. Even if I may have been from a relatively well-to-do family, I've spent 90% of my childhood and my life with a 'tier-2' audience. The middle-class world. That's where I get all the flavors for my videos.

Whenever we make a video in collaboration with or for a brand, we always first start with how will this video relate to that tier-2 audience. Now, we understand it's a difficult task, but we always start with a killer comedy script that has no brand in it. We make a script that's really entertaining for the audience and then we figure out a way to incorporate the brand in it very naturally. Like, it is a paradox. We make a comic script and then find a way to direct it towards the product. So, promotion bhi ho jaata hai, entertainment bhi ho jaata hai. First 50% of the video should be really entertaining, then we introduce the brand.

AP: We all savour a delicious collaboration that elevates the storytelling experience. Dish out the details on your mouth-watering Branded Content projects. How did they make your audience drool with delight? Did you have them at "Product Placement", or was there more to the recipe?

Ashish: We have something really exciting about to launch that I can't divulge yet with one of the global streamers on the brand side – *dil toh karta hai bol daalu, but saala NDA-Ven Dee Ae sign kiya hua hai.* But my voice note to them was clear. We'll all make the money, program toh chal jaayega, but let's make sure we make something epic, yaar, let's get the comedy in place.

I remember, as kids, we used to watch these awesome Fevicol ads. Me, my team, Kunal... we used to trip out on all these. These were the best. Like whoa, what just happened, this was really unexpected, the plot twist. That was an ad? Really? So, we play with that. *Ke saala brand ke kaam aur naam mein bhi mazzaa aa jaye. Yaad rahe!*

My favorite from our work is the one we did for Airtel – you know where the girlfriend is pissed off with her boyfriend because he always takes forever to reply. Up until he gets an Airtel 5G connection when he starts responding instantly. See what I mean? Comedy ki comedy bhi hogayi, aur woh bhi brand ki wajah se [because of the brand]. This reel is our blueprint for all branded content work [Check out Airtel 5G Ashish Chanchlani].

AP: So, when you're hunting for brand partnerships, what ingredients do you look for? How do you whip up a match made in marketing heaven? And most importantly, how do you avoid any awkward flavor clashes when your brand's a vegetarian, and theirs is all about juicy meaty goodness?

Ashish: The first thing we look for is whether we can jam with the founder, key decision maker, the boss at the brand. I meet with them; I need to have a rapport with them. A connection. I need them to understand me, where I come from, where my content originates. 90% of the time it matches, it works. We are really brand friendly. You know, not like bahut brand ka hi kaam karte hain, ya phail jaate hain, but we super service them.

Second, I talk to 4 people from the brand side at different levels with different opinions and see if the joke works across all of them.

If they all laugh, then it's a universal joke. Of course, there are clashes, obviously a loooot of discussions. Sometimes, it can get irritating when some people share an opinion just for the heck of it, woh class participation maarne ke liye. But uss hurdle ko bhi cross karne ke liye humaare paas tareekey hain.

AP: Ah, the never-ending tug-of-war between creative freedom and marketing objectives. It's like squeezing into a tight chef's jacket without breaking a sweat. How do you find that sweet spot that satisfies both your taste buds and the brand's cravings? Any secret culinary formulas you'd like to share?

Ashish: Bahut baar aisa hota hai, we have a lot of jokes but the brand is not happy. I think convincing the brand is the most important and the toughest part of creating Branded Content. It's not shooting, it's not editing, it's not posting, it's not the views. It's the convincing! But if you have the confidence, in yourself, in your comedy or whatever content it is that you create, then they will feel your heart, your soul. If you do it lazily, toh aap pakde jaaoge, they'll catch it, aapki shakal pe dikhega [they'll see it on your face]. That's when the disagreements and discussions begin.

Whenever they disagree, we always take their feedback on board. And we usually over-deliver. If the ask is 2, we land 4. So, there's no scope only left for feedback or a tug-of-war. Mutlab bhar ke... without it becoming on the nose. We tell the brand that the best way to promote the product in the video is to not promote the product. It's like those sea-salt chocolates. The brand call-out should be like that. Public ko chocolate ka sweetness toh mil hi rahaa hai video mein lekin brand ke salt ka ek alag hi mazaa hai.

AP: Behind every mouth-watering Branded Content project lies a recipe for collaboration messier than a dhaba's kitchen. Care to treat us to a sneak peek behind the kitchen doors? What culinary challenges have you faced, and how did you whip them into shape? Did ketchup or any other condiments come to the rescue?

Ashish: Oh, there's a ton of challenges when you're doing a Branded Content piece vs. a traditional content piece where it's your baby, and you have all the creative freedom. To begin with, no below the belt jokes, no offensive jokes, no dark humor, no dank humor, it gets edited out, it goes in the trash even before thinking about it, honestly.

We come up with an idea that will relate to a large middle-class audience. Something that's going on in their lives, something current, trending. Then we write a funny script. And then weave in the brand. We make sure that every funny gag, punch that you watched, that made you laugh in the set up will lead to the brand as a payoff. But also, to break that mould, we sometimes do just the opposite.

Like recently for a tie-in with Renee perfumes, we had such a great time. I loved how they worked with us, how they took feedback, how they understood what we were proposing. Given the target audience of the product, how they wanted to get it into every household... we proposed using the dad-son play-off. And the father-figure character has been such an important recurring character in all my sketches. Dad, dad jokes and the product… all worked so well.

AP: Maintaining the integrity of your content while weaving in a brand's messaging is as delicate as defying gravity with a perfect soufflé. How do you keep it real? How do you ensure the brand integration feels as smooth as a perfectly plated and presented dish?

Ashish: Sirji, the answer to this is simple. Never ever cheat your audience. Never ever take them for granted. They're smart, they're fully updated, they're evolving. You have to keep giving them something fresh. You have to also flood them with 'non-branded' content. These fans, followers, subscribers, they've seen us grow, get bigger. They want the best for us, but also demand the best from us. So, the Entertainment Quotient has to be 90% plus. Even with a paid partnership, you have to ensure the Entertainment lands hard. The youth is the biggest gentry you have. Like now, Gen Z is very different from what we did. I, as a millennial grew up watching Akshay Kumar, Govinda, David Dhawan, Inder Kumar comedy. But now you have to keep yourself up to speed on the latest, hottest trends. You need to have young people around you. And do a lot of research.

AP: The audience holds the power to judge our entertainment choices. How do you gauge their response to your delectable Branded Content projects? Do you have secret spices, feedback

channels, or do you secretly lurk on social media, incognito, to feast on their conversations?

Ashish: Read *all* your comments. *Not just the hard core andhaa/ true fans jo aapse beshumaar pyaar karte hain.* But also, the ones from your casual fans. Who are harder to impress. Take their feedback. I often get on to my stories, channels and ask for feedback. Like recently, for a brand tie-in, for a live stream, what I did is gave my followers, fans a heads-up that this is a brand thing. No bull. No faking. Usually, we pretend and then when people find out this was a plug, they leave your live. So up ahead, I told the community, prepared them, let me make some money, I need it, help me. And they all really appreciated it. The whole narrative changed to, 'Hey what a cool influencer, what a guy!' There were 40,000 people there live, raving. And selling me to the brand!

The cellphone brand and their audience all the way from overseas loved it. They felt it's the most authentic live, beautifully integrated, social engagement they've ever done. Be yourself, be honest, make sure they have fun. And they will always love you.

AP: Alright, time for some creator-to-creator seasoning! Imagine you're mentoring a fresh-faced chef eager to dive into the Branded Content kitchen. What tasty morsels of wisdom would you pass on? What ingredients should they consider before jumping into the culinary embrace of a brand?

Ashish: First, you should have a very strong structure. Irrespective of whether it's a comedy channel, a vlogging channel or whatever your genre. Your base, your script needs to be solid. Phir, don't take too much pressure to promote.

Second, you can't just make it and buzz off. That you've made it, published it, your money is in, ab ghar jaao, mera kaam toh ho gaya [your job is done]. No. You have to see, research, what's working, not working. If it's not working, take the feedback on board. Why didn't the audience like it. Public ko kya achha lag rahaa hai. Accept your mistakes.

Third, create a script in a way that the material works irrespective of the brand. I know this sounds contradictory. But somehow, this is what works for a smooth brand integration.

AP: Based on your experience, what superpowers does Branded Content offer to creators? How does it add flavor to their creative process and extend their reach? Does it come with a snazzy chef's attire and a catchy catchphrase?

Ashish: Mere ko lagta hai ki Branded Content makes you a better creator. My personality has actually improved because of that. You get the confidence to talk to people, convince them. Like chatting with 7 to 8 people, convincing them with confidence about the power of your idea being great... it's a beautiful opportunity. It's a power. That pressure, the deadline from the brand makes your brain run faster. If the brand shares feedback ke, "Mazzaa aa gya", it's such a kick. Like the Airtel team really liked what we'd done. They were delighted. It was such a high. It will definitely change you.

Like the guy that I was in 2017 was so different, that's when I did my first branded reel, and I personally think it was terrible. From there to now... I've gotten so much better.

AP: Let's put on our chef's hats and peer into the crystal ball! What future trends do you see shaping the world of Branded Content? How do you envision the relationship between creators and brands evolving in the years to come?

Ashish: Arre, you can already see it all around you now. Everyone's doing it. And my god, people are so creative. The way people are catching trends, making spoofs, incorporating brands. Some great work... be it some of my peers like Bhuvan [Bam], Carry [Minati]... they're killing it. I get inspired by them. From the new influencers, the superstars of today... a time will come when you won't even come to know that, oh gosh, this was a branded piece. The magician that bridges the brand's message to the people/ audience that only he can – that's a power. It's booming and it's going to get even bigger, it's going to make people's careers and help them buy houses! Samjhe aap?!

EXPERT SPEAK | MEDIA/ STRAT AGENCY PERSPECTIVE: AMIN LAKHANI

Amin is CEO, Mindshare, South Asia and one of the earliest champions of Branded Content. From gently nudging to pushing clients and brands to invest in Branded Content, it was under him that Unilever decided to punt on the multi-award winning 6-Pack Band. He's always been among the first to support the use of tech and innovation in finding creative and content solutions for brands. Evident in the awards for 'Technology Specialist Agency and Mobile Specialist Agency of the Year' at the Goa AdFest, Abby's. Amin shares his views on creating successful Branded Content, so grab your tuxedos, and get ready to infiltrate brand-creator collabs that will shake and stir you!

AP: So, secret agent of collaboration... What role do you play in brokering deals between brands and creators? Are you like the Q of Branded Content, equipping them with the perfect gadgets? And how do you ensure these covert collaborations lead to mission success?

Amin: Branded Content is more about co-creating solutions, than about structuring deals. There is a comprehensive analysis of the brand's goals, target audience, and brand values that needs to be carried out. Followed by the all-important idea generation process where a lot of time and energy is spent into creating the germ, nurturing it and finally giving it a shape and form.

One needs to identify suitable creators, partners or content platforms ensuring creative synergies that resonate with both the brand and the intended audience.

Determining the scope of the collaboration, rights and usage arrangements, compensation structures, and any ancillary benefits is crucial to get a fair and mutually beneficial agreement.

AP: We all love some classified examples. Can you share the top-secret Branded Content campaigns your agency has facilitated? What made these missions stand out in terms of creativity and impact? Did they leave the enemy scratching their heads or just begging for more popcorn?

A good Branded Content campaign

- Is based on consumer truths and trends
- Incorporates pop culture
- And has a deep understanding of the brand proposition and architecture

Some examples of the innovative and impactful work are as follows:

Dove: Thumb-stopping Beauty Biases

Indian women are conditioned from a young age to conform to societal expectations of beauty, which can have a detrimental effect on their self-esteem. A study by Dove revealed that 80% of school-going girls in India face daily assessments of their appearance, which often involve body shaming. This trend has now extended to online platforms, where young individuals engage in conversations with friends, family, and followers.

In response to this social issue, we collaborated with Bobble AI, a popular smart keyboard app in India, to create a real-time intervention. By leveraging contextual AI and predictive technology, the app identifies users who are typing body-shaming comments and sensitizes them to the impact of their words.

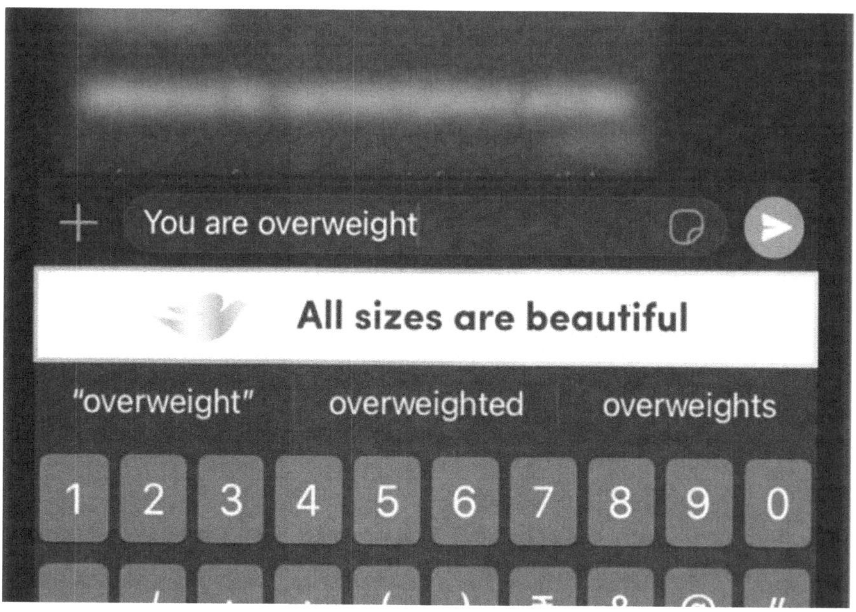

This intervention resulted in an 18% reduction in the usage of body-shaming keywords within just one month. This innovative solution has received recognition at various domestic and international awards, including a bronze prize at the Cannes Lions festival. The intervention serves as a reminder to millions of users that beauty comes in all forms and aims to combat beauty biases one conversation at a time.

Boost: #GameStaminaKa

Boost believes that stamina is the key to success in sports, regardless of gender. To challenge gender-dependent notions in cricket, Boost introduced the world's first gender-equal cricket game, called 'Game of Stamina'. Teaming up with the popular mobile cricket game, 'World Cricket Championship 3', Boost created an immersive gaming experience that highlighted the importance of stamina in determining a cricketer's abilities.

RANK	USER NAME	NET RUN RATES	WINS
1	Whatnext2020	0.793170	4
2	Arvi	4.367589	4
3	GU9408SJW2	0.724277	4
4	ashwin250	1.558213	3
5	Ragufbprod28	0.833333	3
6	Sushash1	4.699080	1
7	Antonyms123	4.078465	1
8	GU3303tB3b	2.994165	1
9	GU6038LLuD	1.000000	1
10	Raineffect	1.000000	1

The game quickly gained popularity, becoming the most-played cricket game across mobile and console platforms during the campaign. Boost successfully engaged its core audience in a medium they frequently use and reshaped perceptions by demonstrating that cricket is not about gender, but about stamina.

Vim: Breaking stereotypes in kitchen and in tech

Vim, India's leading dishwash brand, aimed to challenge gender stereotypes around dishwashing. They launched Vim Black, dishwash liquid for men, which sparked conversations about gender inequity in the kitchen. In reality, there was no Vim Black.

To normalize the role of men in dishwashing, Vim targeted mediums with a higher male audience, such as TV, print, digital, audio, and influencer content. In addition, Vim created a male voice skill for voice assistants like Alexa and Google, providing men with quirky tips and dishwashing hacks from the OG macho man, Milind Soman.

Through these efforts, Vim tackled both kitchen gender bias and technology stereotypes. Despite being a low involvement category, Vim Black initiated discussions about chores and questioned prevailing stereotypes in Indian households.

Cric Exchange: Net Practice for Stock Trading

Upstox, a discount broker in online stock trading, recognized the challenge of helping common Indians understand trading complexities. To address this, they developed Upstox Cric Index in 2020, simplifying the understanding of stock trading. The insight was that people grasp the game better by actually playing it. To bridge the gap from theory to practice, they created Cric Exchange in 2023. This platform allowed users to experience trading and investing through cricket, using players as stocks. With Cric Exchange, users could build their own teams, buy/sell players for portfolio management, and analyse player and team performance. UPruns, a virtual currency, enabled users to practice in a simulated trading world. Cric Exchange became a unique gamified engagement setup in collaboration with Sportz Interactive, Nodwin, BCCI, and Disney+ Hotstar.

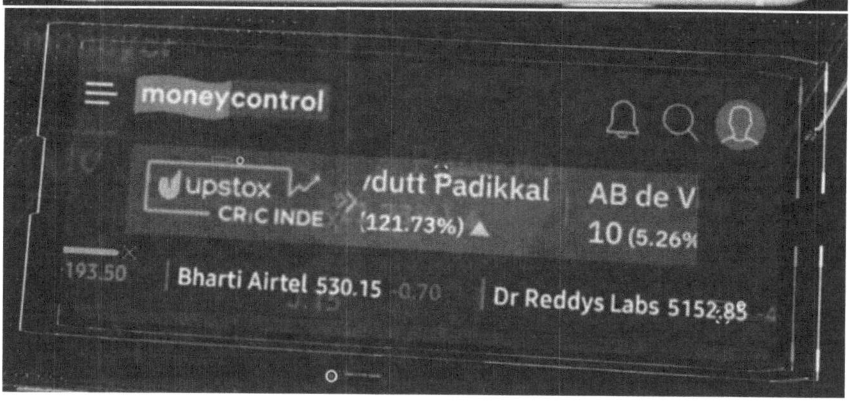

It gained significant attention by hijacking live IPL segments, becoming the official rating system and a discussion point among commentators. Additionally, it garnered consideration by awarding the "Most valuable asset" award to players.

AP: Identifying the right creators or influencers for a brand's target audience is like finding a needle in a stack of exploding

pens. How do you crack the code, Agent X? What criteria do you consider when selecting potential partners for these undercover Branded Content campaigns?

Amin: Simply put, it's a combination of left brain and right brain factors. Creative is really the cornerstone of successful campaigns so we always consider the Creators' past work and their engagement metrics. Other intangibles include their understanding of the brief, their level of enthusiasm. It's not always about the big content creators or the more popular ones but the ones who are big on ideas/ enthusiasm.

We prioritize a data-driven and strategic approach in the selection process. Here's how we do it:

- **Audience demographics:** This helps us gauge the potential reach and resonance of the collaboration.
- **Engagement and influence:** We prioritize those with high engagement rates and genuine influence over their audience.
- **Authenticity and credibility:** We evaluate the creator's authenticity and credibility by considering factors such as their content history, transparency in brand partnerships, and audience perception.
- **Data-driven insights:** We leverage data and analytics tools to gain insights into the performance of creators or influencers. This includes analysing metrics such as audience growth, engagement rates, audience sentiment, and campaign impact. These insights help us make informed decisions based on tangible data.

This approach helps us create authentic connections, maximize reach, and drive meaningful engagement, ultimately delivering successful and impactful campaigns for our clients.

AP: Negotiations and agreements can be riskier than infiltrating a heavily guarded enemy base. How do you ensure a mutually beneficial partnership without blowing your cover? How do you strike a balance between the brand's objectives and the creator's creative freedom, like a true double agent?

Amin: We prioritize several key factors to strike a balance between the brand's objectives and the creator's creative freedom.

- **Alignment of brand values and objectives:** We believe in establishing a strong foundation for any partnership by ensuring that the creator's content aligns with the brand's values and objectives. By working with creators who share a common vision and purpose, we create a foundation that promotes a successful collaboration.

- **Clear guidelines and boundaries:** This includes outlining the key messaging and themes that the brand wants to convey, while also allowing the creator the freedom to infuse their unique creative style into the content.

- **Flexibility and collaboration:** We encourage a process that allows for open discussions, incorporates feedback from both sides, and fosters an environment of continuous improvement.

Having said that, creative freedom results in innovation. We brainstorm on brand briefs with our partners and weave magic, one story at a time!

AP: Measurement is crucial in our line of work. What strategies do you employ to measure the success of your Branded Content missions? Are there invisible ink messages or high-tech gadgets involved? What metrics or performance indicators do you track to evaluate if you're saving the world or just causing an international incident?

Amin: The most important factor we keep in mind is that it has to touch the heart of the consumer. If you don't 'FEEL the IDEA', our consumers will not feel it. The other success criteria are:

- **Brand metrics:** Brand awareness, brand perception, and brand favourability both before and after the campaign.

- **Audience engagement:** Track various engagement metrics that help evaluate the level of interest, involvement, and sentiment generated by the campaign.

- **Content visibility and reach:** The number of impressions, views, and unique users reached across different platforms. This provides insights into the campaign's potential exposure and allows us to gauge the effectiveness of our media planning and buying strategies.

- **Conversion and business impact:** Track key conversion metrics, such as website traffic, lead generation, and sales attribution, to measure the direct impact of the Branded Content campaign on business outcomes. This enables us to evaluate the effectiveness of the campaign in driving tangible results and ROI for our clients.

- **Post-campaign surveys and research:** Conduct surveys and research studies to gather direct feedback from the target audience about their perceptions, recall, and intent to purchase connected to the Branded Content campaign. This qualitative data provides deeper insights into how the campaign has influenced consumer behaviour and attitudes.

- **Awards**: *Work to Win*! Awards are judged by the marketing and media fraternity, and acknowledgement of our peers is very important. *On a lighter note, making the competition jealous is a wonderful metric to chase.*

AP: Staying ahead of the game is essential for spies like us. How do you stay up-to-date with the latest trends and best practices in Branded Content? Are there classified industry resources or intelligence reports you rely on to inform your strategies and decision-making? Or do you have a secret agent hotline?

Amin: Staying up-to-date with the latest trends and best practices in Branded Content is crucial for our agency to maintain thought leadership and deliver innovative solutions to our clients. In short, SEE. HEAR. SHARE.

- **Industry events and conferences:** Actively participate in industry events, conferences, and webinars to stay informed about the latest trends and market dynamics. These gatherings allow us to network with industry professionals, exchange knowledge, and gain insights into emerging practices and technologies.

- **Research and industry reports:** Leverage research studies, market reports, and industry whitepapers to gather data-driven insights and identify key trends. These reports provide a comprehensive understanding of market dynamics and consumer behaviour, allowing us to shape our strategies accordingly.

- **Collaboration with partners and platforms:** Maintain strong relationships with our network of partners, including media platforms, technology providers, and influencers. These collaborations provide us with insights into platform updates, new features, and best practices, enabling us to take advantage of emerging opportunities.

- **Internal learning and development:** Invest in continuous learning and development, fostering a culture of knowledge sharing and upskilling. Through internal training programs, workshops, and knowledge-sharing sessions, we ensure that our team stays abreast of the latest trends and best practices in Branded Content.

- **Data and analytics:** Leverage data and analytics tools, including proprietary tools we use like INCA, to gain insights into creator content performance. Data-driven analysis helps us identify patterns, optimize strategies, and make informed decisions.

Provide our clients with cutting-edge Branded Content solutions that capture audience attention, drive engagement, and deliver impactful results.

AP: Wise words from a seasoned operative! If a brand wants to enter the thrilling world of Branded Content, what advice would you give them? How can they ensure they choose the right agency and extract every bit of intelligence from these partnerships? Should they prepare a disguise kit or bring a suitcase full of untraceable cash?

Amin: For brands looking to enter the world of Branded Content, here is some advice to ensure they choose the right agency and make the most out of these partnerships:

- **Define your goals:** Clearly outline your objectives and goals for the Branded Content campaign. This will help you align with an agency that understands your needs and can tailor their approach accordingly.
- **Evaluate agency capabilities:** Consider the agency's capabilities in planning, buying, digital strategies, content creation, and e-commerce. A comprehensive agency that offers integrated services can provide end-to-end solutions and ensure seamless execution across multiple touchpoints. Assess their expertise in leveraging data, technology, content and analytics to drive insights and measure campaign success.
- **Alignment with brand values**: Ensure that the agency understands and aligns with your brand values and target

audience. Choose an agency that has experience in your industry or understands your target audience's interests. The agency's understanding of your brand and its ability to convey your brand's voice authentically is crucial for successful Branded Content campaigns.

- **Prioritize creative excellence:** Look for an agency that excels in creative execution, storytelling, and producing engaging content. Branded Content is all about creating captivating narratives, so the agency's creative capabilities are pivotal. Seek examples of their previous work to evaluate their creativity, innovation, and ability to deliver compelling content.

- **Measurement and optimization:** Discuss how the agency measures and optimizes the success of Branded Content campaigns. Look for agencies that utilize data-driven insights, employ robust measurement methodologies, and provide regular reporting on key performance indicators. This transparency and data-driven approach will help you understand the campaign's impact and allow for continuous improvement.

- **Foster an ongoing partnership:** Treat your agency as a long-term partner rather than a one-off project. Nurture the relationship by providing feedback, offering insights, and fostering open communication.

AP: Navigating the legal and ethical considerations in Branded Content is like defusing a bomb while juggling glass bowls. How

do you tackle the disclosure and transparency requirements without blowing up the mission? What measures do you take to ensure you're always on the right side of the law, like a spy with a license to thrill?

Amin: Closely monitor the regulatory landscape to ensure our practices align with the latest industry standards and guidelines. Stay up-to-date with relevant laws and regulations, including disclosure requirements, influencer marketing regulations, etc.

One must work closely with legal experts to navigate the legal intricacies and ensure campaigns comply with all applicable regulations.

Work with creators, influencers, and brand partners to ensure that proper disclosures are made, clearly indicating any commercial relationships between brands and creators. And put a robust compliance framework in place that includes regular reviews of campaigns, internal training programs, continuous monitoring, and compliance.

AP: The future is calling! How do you see the landscape of Branded Content evolving in the coming years? Are there any cutting-edge trends or emerging technologies on the horizon that make you want to put on your night-vision goggles and say, *"This is gonna be epic"*?

Amin: Emerging trends and technologies are expected to play a significant role in shaping the future of these collaborations. Here are some key developments to anticipate:

- **Personalization and immersive experiences:** Brands will increasingly leverage technologies such as augmented reality [AR], virtual reality [VR], and mixed reality [MR] to create interactive and engaging content that allows consumers to actively participate and deeply engage with their brand narratives.

- **AI-driven content creation and recommendation:** Artificial intelligence [AI] will play a pivotal role in content creation and recommendation. It will enable more data-driven decisions and enhance the effectiveness of Branded Content campaigns.

- **Integration of voice technology:** Voice technology, including smart speakers and voice assistants, will continue to grow in prominence. Brands will embrace voice-centric Branded Content strategies, creating content and experiences that can be accessed and enjoyed through voice-enabled devices, allowing for seamless brand interactions and increased consumer convenience.

- **Influencer diversification:** As the market becomes more saturated with influencers, we will witness the diversification of influencer partnerships to create more authentic connections and targeted campaigns.

- **The rise of live streaming and real-time interactions:** Live streaming platforms and real-time interactions with audiences will gain even more prominence. Brands can leverage these channels to create immersive live experiences, allowing consumers to engage directly with creators, influencers, and brand ambassadors in an authentic and interactive manner.

- **Sustainability and social responsibility:** Brands and audiences alike are showing increasing interest in sustainable practices and social responsibility. Branded Content campaigns will reflect this by integrating messaging and narratives that align with environmental and social causes, emphasizing the values important to consumers.

- **Data-driven insights and optimization:** The integration of data analytics into Branded Content campaigns will continue to shape the future. Brands will utilize advanced data analysis tools to measure campaign effectiveness, optimize strategies, and deliver hyper-personalized experiences to consumers.

As these trends and emerging technologies continue to evolve, we remain committed to staying at the forefront of Branded Content innovation.

EXPERT SPEAK | CREATOR STUDIO PERSPECTIVE: VIJAY KOSHY

Vijay is President at The Viral Fever [TVF] and a media veteran. Having driven revenue and business for Music Channels, Sports, English Movie clusters, FM Radio Stations and original digital content across the Star Group, Sony, Reliance and Arré, he's seen it and done it in multiple capacities with the scars to prove it. He has played a very key role in scaling up TVF and making it a preferred partner not just for platforms but also for brands to create stories that connect *with consumers. Here we chat about all things content and how to strike a balance while managing a balance sheet when doing that.*

AP: Alright, first things first: Why should brands, and cool folks like you at TVF, give a duck about Branded Content today?

Vijay: With attention spans reducing and the number of brands vying for it increasing, being able to speak with your target audience is becoming harder & harder for brands. Consumers have never been more spoilt for choices with same day deliveries, minute production variations, colour options & many more customisations made to appeal to niches of audience. Attention is now the biggest currency and entertaining content provides this in an undivided & immersive way. If we smartly integrate brands in a way where they do not spoil the audience experience rather compliment it, it's a win-win for everyone.

One of the first few Indian web series that also kickstarted TVF's journey.

AP: Break it down for me, how do you cook up the branded magic at TVF, especially the epic, binge-worthy stuff? Do brands hand you a recipe, or do you match-make ideas with brands? Is it outside in/ inside out... developed based on a brief or pitched after cracking an idea to the right category?

Vijay: All of us consume brands in our daily lives. In fact, many times, we celebrate or wear them on our sleeves with pride. However, our [content] industry somehow looks at them in a manner that they need to be kept away from content in order to protect its sanctity. Maybe it comes from what we now know as the traditional framework for advertising, i.e., keeping ad space or ad airtime separate from editorial or programming air time. At TVF, we look at brands in our content the same way we look at them in real lives, they're tools of convenience all of us desire & hence so do the characters in our stories. Hence, for being able to pull off such work, the first step is to change our outlook.

A lot of our amazing web shows have come from decoding what the target audience in a brand brief would like to watch. We then think what can we make which genuinely entertains this audience while keeping the brand setting at the back of our minds. If one follows this with sincerity then there are millions of untold stories worth being created. Finding a few good ones which both entertain the audience and give an organic platform for brands to feature in shouldn't be impossible.

Additionally, even if we have a story that we want to tell, we focus on the overall arch & takeaway. Remaining fluid on character traits & sub-tracks allows us to adapt aspects within the story which makes the brand's integration very organic.

AP: Let's talk property rights. If the idea comes from a brand's dream and then it lives on, say, Netflix or another platform, not TVF's, who calls dibs on that?

Vijay: Property rights need to be looked at with a lens of what one can benefit from it, instead of the possessive boyfriend approach. It's not a brand's full-time job to make content, they're great at making products & services. Just because they own something, they'll continue investing on it while with the passage of time, newer, more lucrative options might emerge. Continuing to invest on it is then a disservice to its main business. Whereas if a creator owns the property rights, they have the incentive to continue telling that story, bringing in more viewership to the previous episodes made with the brand in question. Since earned media is the objective, then all extra viewership earned due to the creator's commitment to that property is a lot of organic viewership at no further cost.

The basic principle of figuring out each other's objective and proceeding with the most logical solution remains true here too.

AP: How many chef's hats does a brand get to wear in your kitchen? Are they meddling in the script and picking their favorite actors or what? What is the level of involvement they have/ are permitted?

Vijay: Apart from the brand hat, we also look at our brand partners as our first audience. So, we listen to their feedback as carefully as we listen to feedback during internal creative narrations. Genuine feedback is always welcome. In terms of actors, dialogues, jokes and all other creative aspects we seek their trust in *our* creative judgement. We've found most brand folks to be extremely understanding & supportive here.

AP: Alongside the killer content, what other goodies do you hand over? I mean, is there a spreadsheet tucked under the storyboard? Views/ reach commitments/ social media call-outs/ other?

Vijay: Yes, of course, we're much more into excel sheets than one would imagine. The kind of content we're focused on making does require decent investment. Views is as much a barometer for audience reception as it is a measurement for brands, so we do include that in our excels. Over the years, we've also earned a huge following across our 4 channels – TVF, Timeliners, Girliyapa & Screen Patti, cumulatively stacking up above 50 mn. So, we build a robust organic plan around each content asset to ensure it gets the right number of eyeballs and a fair chance to strike virality.

AP: Beyond likes, shares, and my mom watching – are there any business-y metrics or numbers you're eyeballing when the content rolls out?

Vijay: Surprised, since my mom is still watching Satellite TV. On a more serious note, however, each brand has a different way of measuring ROI. For early-stage brands, its easiest since such activities move almost all their needles. For mature brands, one must understand that they sit on a huge base and years of brand positioning and reinforcing has created a firm imagery. To create substantial movements on that is a difficult exercise requiring concerted long-term efforts. That said our experience has been that branded content has been extremely adept in achieving these movements. These movements are measured via brand tracks or A/B brand lift studies to ratify the directional movement & decide future course of action.

AP: Rupya, dhandhaa, dollar bills! What's the price tag sweet spot where brands are like, 'Shut up and take my money,' and you guys are like, 'Deal!'? Do you have a menu with prices?

Vijay: As we know, a meme is content and the whole of MCU [Marvel Cinematic Universe] is also content. It's a rather broad word comprising so many formats and possible scales. So, yes, we do have a menu, but we only use it as a guideline to help brand partners visualise possibilities and skip jump to what seems possible to them given their overall plans. There is as such no sweet spot, the investment that brand makes is a function of the problem they're trying to address with it. A consumer behaviour problem affecting brand sales cannot be equated to a sales campaign, the former would require years of impactful cultural work while the latter is tactical.

AP: Alright, show-off time! Give me your top 3 show-stoppers in Branded Content from TVF's vault.

Vijay: Hard to choose 3 – every person you'll ask at TVF will have a different combination. Mine however is, Kota Factory, a black &

white web show about the assembly line approach to churning young students that became one of the most watched Indian web shows of all time, rated amongst the Top 100 IMDB Shows Globally and also did an amazing job of bringing out Unacademy's core proposition of aiding IIT JEE Students in prepping for the test.

Yeh Meri Family – family life from the 90s so authentically & lovingly presented from a 12-year old's POV, each episode strikes a chord. This is another branded show from TVF which features in the IMDB Global Top 250 shows of all time. This show brings out mutual fund education seamlessly via the father who depicts a financial planner and calmly through superb analogies explains the right way to approach investments.

And Tripling, a road trip of siblings so cool & deeply entrenched in culture that it triggered a hashtag used till date by siblings on trips. This brand partnership also happened at a very sensitive time when Tata Motors had launched one of its most important cars, the Tiago. Tripling played a very key part in helping improve youth appeal for this car. Tiago remains one of the best-selling Tata cars till date.

AP: Spread the love – any 2 branded masterpieces out there not by TVF that made you a teensy bit jealous?

Vijay: Coke Studio, the sound it has created & maintained and Coke's commitment to it. Overall, the kind of work Red Bull does, jumping from space being the highlight of it. And the most recent one is Barbie, amazing success with audience and if it was constructed on a brief then it seems to have checked all the boxes.

AP: So, even the best fall down sometimes. Got a tale of a branded dud? What did that teach you? How will you avoid that the next time around? Spill!

Vijay: There are so many things that can go wrong in content creation. Things can get lost in translation from idea to screenplay to final edit by any one team and the final product can miss the mark even with the best of the intentions. I wouldn't call it exactly a dud but 'Bisht Please', something we did with Snapdeal got about 12 million views across 6 episodes, while we were expecting much more. We've tried to minimize this to the lowest by building a culture of feedback within the organisation. We encourage everyone to speak up and give candid feedback. At the same time, we encourage writers & directors to be open to feedback. This helps ensure that someone in the chain speaks up & helps course correct before it's too late.

AP: When brands want their name in, well, bigger neon lights, how do you keep the content from looking like a billboard?

Vijay: Most brands don't bother as long as its well-presented. Very few times this gets debated, however, we keep coming back to the key reason of this partnership, i.e., to earn audience attention first and then use that as a platform to communicate the brand message. That plus given the number of successful case studies we have, we're quite persuasive.

AP: Time for a quick-fire round! Three must-dos for brands itching to dive into the Branded Content pool?

Vijay: Well, [1] Understand that advertising framework cannot be applied to content. If you're going to make content where you're having to buy views then you might as well make another ad or use that money to buy more views on existing ads. Work with creators whose content creation skills you admire, brief them well & then trust them to deliver.

[2] Evaluate content partners on TG fit & creation abilities. Most brands make the mistake of going idea first. A decent idea can come from couple of hours of jamming and a great deck-designer. Amazing content, however, is hundreds of people working tirelessly

for months. So, a good idea in itself is useless unless it's backed by that level of creation ability.

[3] Understand the budgets required and the entitlements upfront. No use spending weeks or months evaluating ideas without doing a basic check on what something would broadly cost. Most creators with experience can help get a rough idea of that with barely any effort.

AP: And for my creative comrades looking to clinch these branded deals – three golden nuggets of advice? How do they seal the deal without selling their soul?

Vijay: [1] Understand the brand's brief very well. Never assume what they want based on your perception of their brand.

[2] Be fair, look for a win-win. Creative solutions exist & people wanting to put the work in will find them.

[3] Imbibe the brand in your narrative, don't try to hide it under the carpet. Brand partners will figure out intent faster than you think.

AP: When you kick back and look at a branded piece, how do you toast to its success? What's the victory dance metric?

Vijay: Views, audience love in comments, audience love across platforms [Half CA generated thousands of LinkedIn appreciation posts], IMDB ratings & rankings but most of all, whether the brand partner is happy or not.

AP: Whip out your crystal ball. Where's Branded Content headed? Are we talking VR, space billboards or season 83 of Tripling?

Vijay: As a storytelling organisation, we know stories have always existed and always will. The platform or formats keep changing as technological advancements take place. But the base principle remains the same, audiences want to be entertained and we want to keep entertaining them [format no bar].

EXPERT SPEAK | CREATIVE/ STRAT AGENCY PERSPECTIVE: DHEERAJ SINHA

Dheeraj is Group CEO, FCB India and South Asia. When we did this interview, he was CEO, Leo Burnett, South Asia and Chairman, BBH India. He's been strategy and planning head across agencies like Grey, Bates, McCann Erickson and is one of the most respected names in Indian Advertising. A MICA grad, and author of multiple books; under his charge, his team has picked up tons of awards at the GoaFest including Creative Agency of the Year, Branded Entertainment Agency of the Year and more. And most recently #1 Indian Agency at Cannes. They've done some incredible work across brands including Spotify, Pepsi, Mondelez, P&G and in the Health Sector. Here, he shares his learnings on working with brands to hack and crack Branded Content.

AP: Alright, so why do you think, if at all, that branded content is essential today?

Dheeraj: I think the biggest aspect of marketing and brand building which has never been quoted in any of the books of Kotler or anyone is the need for entertainment. My analogy is that you have a child and you want give the child a bitter pill. Would you rather coat it in chocolate so that it goes in, or would you rather give her a bitter pill to swallow as is which she resists. Say 30 or 40 years back when Television advertising was invented, or when the idea of 'Unique Selling Proposition' was invented, we had attention as a given. And therefore, all or most marketing models do not have attention as any of the pillars. So, you think about consumer, you think about differentiation, you think about what you have to say. It's so inward driven. If you look at ALL the marketing models, they're about us. They're not about the audience. I think even the AIDA model, is still very focused on what WE have to say. Consumers don't care for what you have to say. In the days when you had one channel in most countries or two channels at best, the channels had the authority over what you can watch.

And now, cut to the 2000s, when everybody has a mobile phone, that's entertainment on the go, everybody's a creator, right? Attention is the biggest thing to get. Entertainment therefore becomes the biggest rocket, so to say, to ride your payload. And therefore, single-most critical thing for marketing today, for business today, if you're investing any money in media is to get attention. And therefore, Branded Content comes into play.

Second, I think there's HUGE suspicion from people of paid advertising. So, you know, you get a huge celebrity and people say, Amitabh Bachchan is saying this because we paid the money. I think people are smart today. They know it. Things have been published. I mean, a common lay consumer now knows how much a celebrity charges for an ad. That data was never public. Today that data is public. Everybody knows what Virat Kohli charges for an Instagram post. So, there's huge suspicion of paid advertising. But if there's some piece of entertainment that I'm enjoying, and I'm really loving it with my family, my friends and the brand happens to be part of that narrative, I, at least, register it. And if I like it, I say, yeah, these guys are cool. I want to hang out with them. So, you still get a concession that ok, there is something in it for me. You're being funny, or you're being entertaining.

From an agency lens, I think it's the best time to be in advertising because you are no longer limited by formats, you don't have to think in 30 second TVCs or print layouts. Your palette can be as wide as your imagination allows you. You can launch a campaign through a press conference like the Oreo relaunch with Dhoni, through content, through whatever you want.

AP: A lot of times one gets briefs saying, 'Give us something with AI' or 'a tech innovation for awards' like those days of 'viral video chahiye'. A lot of the work that you've done integrates tech as a layer so seamlessly. At what stage does this tech come in and what role does it play?

Dheeraj: The idea is to build a culture so that the system begins to think, generate like that. Two pieces like that will happen because you personally have your hands in it. You will never have 20 pieces unless the system starts to generate it.

I'm NOT in the IT consulting business. I'm NOT in a data business. Everything that we do is in the service of creativity which helps businesses succeed and which solves problems for people. I've never been clearer about this in my life. Now, whether it's tech, data or branded content, everything comes to make creativity come alive.

When we were working on the Airtel 83 campaign, the objective was to make something like 5G intelligible to an audience as wide and varied as India. Typically, when you launch a service like that, the ads are, Grandfather talking to the Grandchild on an iPad, enabled by 5G. So, we thought, what if the technology of the future actually enables us to get hold of our history. We tapped into nostalgia. The Kapil Dev 175 knock which was never recorded, telecast. What if we recreate that match. And 5G enables us to experience that in all its glory.

Then came the mammoth part of connecting with people who can help us de-age Kapil, recreate that environment, do a hologram of Kapil, the arena, all of it. Tech becomes an execution piece. But the whole idea is creativity led. We never start with saying, ok, let's do something with AI. Never. And we will never do that.

AP: Finding the perfect creator or influencer for a brand's target audience is like finding a needle in a haystack made of hashtags. How do you crack that code? What criteria do you use to select the potential partners for these Branded Content campaigns? Do you have a superpowered algorithm? I remember one of your partner agencies who worked on that Airtel/ Kapil 175 campaign going completely cuckoo trying to figure out how to do this...

Dheeraj: Oh, I had a lot more black hair before this campaign!

My guiding philosophy on everything is always go to best in class. For the Kapil campaign, we identified 'Double Negative'. As a team they'd worked on the 'Dune' movie, picked up Golden Globes, Oscars. Depending on budgets, availability, we work with people who are doing a lot of Avant Garde work. There's a lot of those skill sets in India as well. The HP Lubricants' Roads that Honk was done out of India. A lot of the new Mondelez work is being done from within the Publicis Group as we're developing, building up that skillset inhouse now.

We need people who are willing to learn with us. Seeking partnerships. Advertising has historically been a very silo-ed function. Egos came before ideas. We've systematically dismantled the egos. We believe it takes a village. A 100-plus people to create something spectacular. So, we are hungry for that kind of collaboration. From within and outside. That's what is helping us a lot.

AP: Negotiations and agreements can be more intense than a stare-down between Wolverine and Hulk. How do you ensure a win-win situation for both brands and creators? How do you find that sweet spot where the brand's objectives and the creator's creative freedom dance the tango without stepping on each other's toes?

Dheeraj: That's the job of a business leader. Or a strategist. You have to continuously remind the 20 people in the room that we're getting paid to create this. But the millions of people outside this room have no stake in this. Why will they watch this? Just because you're saying it? So, every meeting, I have to remind people. We are triple-filtered MBAs. We may have studied the frameworks but people won't see the PowerPoint behind the work. They won't know the models behind the work. Nobody will register it. That has to be a constant reminder.

Even telling the client that we can say what you're asking us to, but will it help you? And it's not a one-time thing. It's a continuous conversation. Every time we've managed to push through something spectacular, we've had to navigate that in a very very big way. And once a set of people see that it works, then it becomes easier to push through. There will always be a first time, there will always be a pushback, because we've all become very polluted. Having spent 20 lakhs or so on MBAs, we've at times lost the ability to connect things. So, it has to be reiterated in every meeting.

From a creativity standpoint, I'm very clear that this is a commercial art. We are not here to pander to our personal desires. If you think you're a great art person, please go home and paint. You think you're a fantastic writer, go home, write poetry, write a film. To suit or satisfy your personal creative instincts. But when we are at work, when we are using client money, our only religion is to solve for a client's business problems, to get her a promotion. That is the only service we are in. We are brutally clear about it.

AP: We all love some show-stopping examples. Give us the 3 juiciest campaigns you love. That were kickass creatives, solved client problems, and just stood out. In different categories, formats. What made these babies stand out from the crowd in

terms of creativity and impact? Did you have the world screaming, "Encore!" or maybe just "More popcorn!"

Dheeraj: I'd go way back, Ashiish, to something that I did not do over here, but a long time back. The 'Indian Pangaa League' for Virgin Mobile. 40 to 50 commercials, shot under a crore, on a CanonD, written by 100 people from within the agency, went on YouTube without any promotions and just went viral. I remember I got a call from my wife that there were people playing this in her office, that's when I realized that this is going somewhere. Those days there were no theories, no frameworks, experimenting with instincts. Today people talk about context specific content. We did this when it was far ahead of its time. One piece always close to my heart.

Second, I'd say, Airtel 175. Because of the connections we made. I mean who launches a technology of the future by bringing a piece of history back, [A]. And [B], it's a long form, and the execution was mindboggling. And to get that done for the first time, I had to get down, to deep granularity on how the CG works. How is this made, 12 computers to render, linear, you can't speed it up. 10 days before launch I got shots of Kapil that didn't look like Kapil [laughs]. But we pulled it off.

Third, is a traditional piece. The Spotify IPL films. We broke the format of classical storytelling, there are no dialogues, only music. Anytime we play it anywhere in the world, everyone just gets it, laughs. You know TV is so looked down upon as being too traditional. We broke all the 'traditional' structures of problem, one dialogue, product window, solution, logo. So that's why.

And all of these pieces have worked for the brand and the business. They're not indulgences. They've moved the needle for the product and got the people on the brand's side promoted. Besides picking up a ton of awards.

Outside of our own, the Shahrukh Khan Mondelez/ Cadbury Diwali campaign was a great piece of work. And a lot of the Ryan Reynolds work.

AP: Every hero faces their fair share of obstacles. What challenges have you encountered while playing matchmaker between brands and creators? And how did you conquer these hurdles to ensure a partnership that's smoother than a well-greased spandex suit? Did you call in the Avengers for backup?

Dheeraj: Lots of pieces like that. We were doing some work for HDFC Life. We wanted to build birthday cakes that looked like pie charts. Based on data of how you spend your time. For retirement plans. To remind them about how they spend their time matters. And we couldn't execute it the way we would have wanted.

What I have realised in life is that the connections on things have to be very simple. They have to be thought from people out rather than us out. Because we have such intelligent people on our side that we can complicate things. We build layers that no one is able to decipher. So many times, things do not work because no one could understand it. It just didn't land because people didn't get it. People don't want to sit and pontificate and decipher what we have to say. All the work we do has to have a low cognition load on people. So, our connections have to be very very simple. Most of our efforts fail when the connections are not simple enough.

Second, is execution, execution, execution. You may have a great idea but if you're not able to execute it with great craft, then you're gone.

Those are biggest things that we watch out for in a very sharp way.

AP: Measurement is the name of the game! How do you gauge the success of your Branded Content campaigns? Are there secret strategies up your sleeve? What metrics or performance indicators do you track to evaluate if you're hitting the bullseye or just hitting yourself in the face with a pie?

Dheeraj: Everything we think is to solve for a business problem. Nothing for the heck of it. No, 'This brand is about this, let's celebrate this for the brand'. Nothing that's generic brand building... nothing that doesn't move the business. The Oreo relaunch with Dhoni moved business, moved penetration. It's moved 45% as of date on sales growth, it helped 5 basis points penetration go deeper. The Airtel 175 piece has helped launched 5G very successfully. So, everything we do is to solve for a business problem. When we did the 'Bring the Missing Chapter back' for P&G's Whisper... It was to keep girls in school. And the data has already started moving, leading to sales of Whisper. That's the first and foremost premise.

Of course, on all brands we have sales metrics, usage metrics, download metrics, depending on the category. We measure all of that. All of these cases are effectiveness awards winners as well.

Because we've delivered on Brand, Business and Social metrics. We measure all 3. You'll always know whether it's worked or not.

My only submission is if we begin to design everything to solve for a business problem, then it just becomes clear. The results would be far better.

AP: Staying ahead of the game is crucial in this fast-paced world. How do you stay up-to-date with the latest trends and best practices in Branded Content? Are there secret industry hangouts or mystical sources of wisdom you rely on? Do you have a hotline to the marketing gods?

Dheeraj: It's very organic and intuitive. I wouldn't say that all 600 to 700 folks at Leo Burnett do it. But the curious ones do it. We're always plugged into...

- Contagious – a great source of what's going around in the world.
- Fast Company – I try and get to the Fast Company Innovation conference in New York every year to see/ feel the temperature.
- Cannes – my creative partner, Raj, is a walking/ talking encyclopaedia of the work there, in his mind everything is catalogued.

In our agency, the ask is if you're sitting to brief, or think of a brief, you have to play in that meeting what is the benchmark work in that category. Now ask, how do we beat this. For this audience. For this category. For this brand.

Also, we get our creative directors to run some sessions on interesting stuff. But nothing beyond that. The culture is that if you're not cued in, with the references being spoken about, you'll just feel really left out. I mean, we've hired people from other agencies and they're very good strategic planners. But they've never seen or had the appreciation of seeing work. So, I always tell them, if you have two months before you join us, go and devour all the great work out there.

I was in MICA [Mudra Institute of Communication Arts, Ahmedabad] and I barely attended classes. I wish I had. But all I did was, get in the library, with headphones, check out all the best work that was being done globally on those VHS tapes. Read all the books I could. That's all I remember of MICA.

I'm always curious, what is Ryan Reynolds doing. What is someone else doing. We have a call every Tuesday with 50 of our top leaders. We're always talking about – here's what they're doing, what are we doing? That's the conversational currency on the floor at the agency.

Ashiish, we would spend the same time to do work which is 3 on 10 as we'd do for something which is an 8 on 10. Our lives are what our lives are. None of us are getting younger. I'm probably getting older faster [laughs]. Welcome to advertising! What do you want to spend that time doing?

AP: Wise words time! If a brand wants to enter the enchanting world of Branded Content, what advice would you give them? How can they find the right agency and squeeze every drop of magic out of these partnerships? Should they bring their lucky charm or offer you a lifetime supply of chimichangas?

Dheeraj: There's a lot of need for unlearning for marketers. And also, for agencies. The art of letting go. The broadcast medium is about saying what you want to say. And the entertainment medium is about influencing the narrative. Both the arts/ sciences are very different. That's the first learning/ or unlearning.

You want to make a TVC, it's dictated by what message you want to put out, your brand name will come 6 times, you'll end with a baseline, this is all dictated by you. A piece of entertainment should not be dictated by you. You'll spoil it.

We're all called Brand 'Managers'. The entire function has been designed around 'managing' and 'controlling'. And entertainment means letting go of control. It's the antithesis of what we've been taught.

Secondly, you have to work with best in class. How it starts, where it ends will be very different if you don't work with the right partners who get you, who get the brand, who know their stuff. People who obsess about the end product.

And thirdly, I'd reiterate that everything should be to the service of solving for a business problem.

AP: Legal and ethical considerations are like a supervillain waiting to strike. How do you navigate the treacherous waters of disclosure and transparency in Branded Content? What measures do you take to ensure you're a law-abiding hero, not a mischievous villain plotting world domination? Especially in today's woke world.

Dheeraj: This gets covered/ discussed, at a strategic and creative level. For instance, the idea to cast Ishaan Khatter and Anil Kapoor for Spotify happened not at execution/ casting level but at a strategic level. To bring in the generational gap. Anil had not been seen for a while; at that time, he was not so visible. Ishaan was not that big that time. So, these things you do up ahead. Which help.

Of course, you watch out for clauses, usage, compliance, legalese during execution. Having said all of that, mistakes happen Ashiish. You're dealing with things that are volatile. Celebrities, context, content. And it's very easy in retrospect to say we messed up. No one wakes up in the morning to plan to make a mistake. Despite the best of your efforts, mistakes will happen. There is no foolproof way to prevent it.

Then, there comes the time to figure... Are you willing to walk that path of fire with your partner or will you jettison them. You have to be in it together to salvage it.

AP: The future is calling! How do you see the landscape of Branded Content evolving in the coming years? Are there any mind-blowing trends or emerging technologies on the horizon that

make you want to grab a bucket of popcorn and jump on the nearest unicorn?

Dheeraj: My ambition and my desire is that everything becomes branded content. That we learn to not make it in the face. That it is paid for. But doesn't look paid for. We still have a journey to cover there. But there's no stopping it. It's going to be omnipresent.

Inherently, <u>advertising has to become 'playable'. Stuff you can play with</u>.

AP: Any parting words... for readers, leaders, students, for people getting into this world of Branded Content.

Dheeraj: I have only one ask. See everything from people's perspective. We are getting paid to create this. No one is getting paid to watch this.

Keep that in mind all the time.

THE FUTURE OF BRANDED CONTENT

Everything changes all the time. So, to try and look into a crystal ball and predict the future is as smart as trying to figure out what Ranveer Singh will wear or Urfi Javed won't wear to their next public appearance. But one thing is certain, the future of Branded Content is as bright as a supernova wearing sunglasses. As audiences continue to evolve and traditional advertising loses its grip on their attention, branded content will step in like a cool, smooth-talking hero to save the day.

Here's a glimpse into what the future potentially holds:

1. **Seamless Integration:** Branded Content will seamlessly integrate into our lives like a chameleon at a disco. It will infiltrate various forms of media, blurring the lines between entertainment and advertising. From movies and TV shows to social media and video games, brands will cleverly weave themselves into the fabric of our experiences without interrupting the fun.

2. **Interactive Experiences:** Audiences will no longer be mere spectators but active participants in the Branded Content universe. They'll dive into immersive experiences, unlock hidden storylines, and influence the outcome of narratives. It's like being the hero in your own action-packed movie, where the choices you make shape the plot. Content will no longer be just what you see or hear, but it will be what you do as well.

3. **Personalized Content:** Brands will tap into the power of data and AI to deliver hyper-personalized content that feels tailor-made for each individual. It's like having a personal genie who knows exactly what tickles your fancy. By understanding audience preferences, behaviours, and interests, branded entertainment will serve up content that resonates on a deeply personal level. 'Joan is Awful?' Ouch!

4. **Collaborations and Co-Creation:** The future will see an explosion of collaborations between brands, creators, and influencers. They'll join forces to create captivating content that combines the strengths of different worlds. It's like mixing peanut butter with jelly to create a taste sensation that leaves

your taste buds begging for more. By pooling resources and creativity, brands will unlock new dimensions of entertainment.

As a side-note, for some brands, it will also mean investing/ buying out/ acquiring some content creators or communities as a shortcut to skill up.

5. **Cause-Driven Storytelling:** Branded Content will champion important causes and tackle social issues with the force of a hurricane with a heart. Brands will use their influence to drive positive change, promoting inclusivity, diversity, sustainability, and social justice. It's like a superhero fighting for a better world, using storytelling to inspire and ignite action. This is going to be not just an opportunity but a responsibility for brands. Not just to hack an awards show, but to genuinely make a difference.

6. **Immersive Technologies:** Virtual reality [VR], augmented reality [AR], and other immersive technologies will transport audiences to breath-taking realms. Brands will create immersive experiences that go beyond the screen. Like stepping into a portal that takes you to a world where possibilities are endless.

7. **Data-Driven Insights:** Brands will harness the power of data analytics to gain deeper insights into audience behaviour and preferences. By understanding audience reactions and sentiments, brands can fine-tune their content to deliver even more impactful experiences.

8. **Multiplatform Distribution:** Branded Content will break free from traditional platforms and explore new avenues of distribution. It will roam freely like a wild stallion, accessible across multiple platforms and devices. From streaming services to social media platforms to emerging technologies, Branded Content will be omnipresent, capturing attention wherever audiences roam.

9. **Authentic Storytelling:** Authenticity will be the guiding star of branded content. Brands will embrace vulnerability, transparency, and genuine connections with their audience. It's like having a heart-to-heart conversation with a trusted friend. By telling stories that resonate on a human level, brands will forge deep emotional bonds with their audience.

10. **Endless Innovation:** The future of branded content will be a cauldron of innovation, constantly bubbling with new ideas and technologies. Brands will push the boundaries of storytelling, experimenting with unconventional formats, emerging technologies, and mind-bending narratives.

Some things never change. Yeah, seriously. It's like the universe has a wicked sense of humor.

No matter what futuristic wonders we conjure up, people will forever yearn for improvement. They'll always want things faster, better, and cheaper. It's like a cosmic itch they can't help but scratch. We might be rocking hoverboards and robot butlers in the near future, but deep down, we'll still be craving those sweet upgrades.

Humans will forever hunger for education, entertainment, and emotional engagement. Yup, even in a world where we can teleport to Mars for a Sunday brunch. You see, no matter how advanced we get, we'll always crave that spark that lights up our souls, that connection that makes us feel alive. It's just the way we're wired, and hey, who am I to argue with human nature?

Stay curious, stay entertained, and always keep that gleam in your eye.

The possibilities are endless, and the future is waiting to be entertained.

THE NEW BOSS IN TOWN

Well, well, well, look who's about to graduate from Branded Content School! Congrats, you magnificent genius, you! Trust me, it's practically a golden ticket to success.

I sure hope I managed to lend a hand along the way. Did you learn a thing or two about Branded Content? Did your brain cells do a happy little dance? I like to think I had something to do with that. But hey, no pressure. If you didn't, just blame it on some cosmic hiccup or your kundali bhagya. It's a foolproof excuse, and I won't hold it against you.

Now, if you enjoyed this wild ride of a book, please spread the word! Share the juicy details, shout it from the rooftops, and let the world know that Branded Content has a new boss in town. Reviews, my friends, reviews! Give it a glowing recommendation if it tickled your fancy. I mean, who wouldn't want to follow in your stylish footsteps?

And as you embark on this new chapter as a certified Branded Content Boss, may the universe bless you with all the good fortune and opportunity you can handle. Grab life by the metaphorical horns, wrangle those branded beasts, and show 'em who's boss!

Alright, champ, it's time for you to shine. Go forth and conquer the world of Branded Content like the superhero I know you are. And remember, when in doubt, just ask yourself: What would the Branded Content Boss do? That should solve any dilemma.

Stay awesome, keep rocking those branded socks, and keep making the world a better place, one entertaining brand at a time. Go get 'em, tiger!

Ashiish V Patil, out!

RESOURCES & TEMPLATES

Fellow hustlers... Life moves fast. And Branded Content faster. And let's face it, real bosses never stop skilling so they can continue killing it. But here's the funny thing: there aren't a ton of resources out there specifically for Branded Content. That's why I decided to create this book in the first place. But learning can come from a variety of sources, even if not directly related.

Here are a few things you can do to continue your learning journey...

1. **Books:** I used to be intimated by books, but then someone told me something that changed my life forever, *"Those who don't read are no better than those who can't read."* Reading is the number one way to learn. It's your own pace, your own space to dive deep, understand, access the wisdom of experts you might not meet otherwise. And the best part? It's way cheaper than other tools out there. Sadly, I couldn't find anything specifically in the Indian context, but here are a few books to get you started.

Everybody Writes: Your Go-To-Guide to Creating Ridiculously Good Content by Ann Hadley

One of the most respected names in content marketing, Ann is also the founder of MarketingProfs.com. It's filled with practical tips, great examples and her signature sense of humor and is a great place to start.

Epic Content Marketing: How to Tell a Different Story, Break through the Clutter, and Win More Customers by Marketing Less by Joe Pulizzi

Fortune Magazine ranked this as a Top 5 Must-Read Business Book. Packed with insights on content marketing vision, case studies, measuring effectiveness. Now, there's a new edition out covering content and community building in Web3.

Storynomics: Story-Driven Marketing in the Post-Advertising World by Robert McKee and Thomas Gerace

Robert is a big shot in Hollywood as a screenplay coach and his alumni list is off-the-charts with Academy Award, Golden Globe, Emmy winners. Thomas runs a content marketing unit called Skyword. This book combines the art of storytelling with marketing strategies showing you the power of narrative to engage audiences.

Creativity Inc. by Ed Catmull

Forbes Magazine said 'Just might be the best business book ever written'. Ed, the President of Pixar and Disney Animation Studios known for blockbuster films including Toy Story, Up, Finding Nemo and more. It's part biography, part Pixar history, part business book, but it's a fab manual for anyone hoping to build, sustain a creative culture, and figure how to work with creative people.

Making Movies by Sidney Lumet

Roger Ebert, the legendary film critic, said, *"If there's one book a filmgoer could read to learn more about how movies are made and what to look for while watching them. This is the book."* While it's about feature films and filmmaking, it's a fantastic resource to understand the craft and all its elements.

2. **Courses:** While researching for this book, I scoured the internet and found a few content marketing courses but felt they didn't quite scratch the Branded Content itch. Most were focused on social media, digital marketing or part of a larger module with not enough width or depth on Branded Content. This was across Coursera, Skillshare, Udemy, Futurelearn internationally and UpGrad, Whistling Woods, Simplilearn, Digital Vidya, SP Jain School of Global Management, Indian School of Business in India. Fortunately, there's a wide variety of courses available online on different storytelling formats from films, fiction, docus, poetry, lyrics, series to first solidify the entertainment side, then bring in the branding.

These are some that you should surely check out.

Writing for Television by Shonda Rhimes on Masterclass

The lady behind some of TV's biggest and most talked about hits from Grey's Anatomy, Scandal and more. Fantastic teacher, no nonsense style, practical tips on working a writer's room and craft.

Screenwriting by Aaron Sorkin on Masterclass

Oscar Winner, writer, director, the man behind films like The Social Network, A Few Good Men, the Steve Jobs biopic, shows like West Wing and arguably one of the best dialogue writers in the business.

Screenwriting by Varun Grover on Frontrow

Varun is a multi-talented gem – lyricist, screenwriter, graphic novelist, stand-up comedian and an awesome teacher. The course is great as it's among the few with Indian storytelling references.

Lyric-writing by Swanand Kirkire on Frontrow

Actor, writer, lyricist, Swanand knows how to write words that stick to your brand like glue. The man behind some of Bollywood's most memorable songs like those from '3 Idiots', 'English Vinglish', 'Munnabhai MBBS', 'Kai Po Chhe'. Plus, he's no stranger to brand work, so you're in for a treat.

Writing and Performing Poetry by Amanda Gorman on Masterclass

The First National Youth Poet Laureate, brought down the house with her iconic reading of 'The Hill We Climb' at the 2021 Biden inauguration. She's not only a poetic powerhouse but also an author of three incredible books.

Creative Writing Course by Jerry Jenkins

The king of the writing realm with over 200 books across genres and a staggering 73 million plus copies sold. That's like having your own personal writing mentor guiding you through the wild jungles of creativity. Oh, and did I mention, he has a treasure trove of free resources?

Writing Under Pressure by Dan Nelken

Dan is an advertising guru and he knows how to pack a punch with his quick, fun, and actionable tips. This particular course focuses on fast and thoughtful headline creation.

3. **Newsletters/Blogs/Websites:** Internationally, content marketing has matured a lot more and there are a few websites, blogs that you can subscribe to which have a wealth of information.

Content Marketing Institute [CMI]

The Jedi masters of content marketing, offering a range of events; training programs and articles, expert interviews, best practices. https://contentmarketinginstitute.com/

HubSpot Blog

HubSpot, the marketing software giant has a blog that covers various topics including Branded Content, storytelling, social media, and more. https://blog.hubspot.com/marketing

Adweek

The trusted source of news and insights for the advertising and marketing industry. Their website and weekly newsletter are your ticket to staying on top of the hottest new campaigns and trends, analysis from industry experts. https://www.adweek.com/

Contently.com

This site is the holy grail of all things content. From a creative marketplace to tech solutions and case studies. One of the founders is Shane Snow, a former journalist, entrepreneur and content marketing expert, author, who has also written for Wired and is considered the real deal. https://contently.com/

Social Samosa

A leading Indian digital marketing publication that covers various aspects of marketing including content marketing and branded content. They're more focused on the digital/ social side, but given everything today has a social leg, it's a must-have resource. https://www.socialsamosa.com

4. **Awards:** Some of the big advertising/ marketing awards round the world have now had no choice but to introduce a Branded Content category. Examples of people who've won these shiny

trophies of recognition over the years will help you make your brand shine brighter than the sun.

Cannes Lions

The best of the best. It recognises the best work across categories including branded entertainment and content and several of the case studies featured in this book are winners of multiple Cannes Lions. Winning one of these babies is like being knighted by the creative gods themselves.

D&AD Awards

Considered to be one of the most prestigious in the design and advertising industry, they feature outstanding creative work across various categories including Branded Content.

Effie Awards

The champions of marketing campaigns that pack a punch and achieve their goals. They cover everything including branded content and entertainment.

Webby Awards

The internet's playground of outstanding work. It's where the coolest cats in the digital world gather to celebrate mind-boggling creativity. These awards are a window into the coolest tech innovations and trends also in advertising and marketing.

GoaFest

The ultimate celebration of Indian advertising. Hosted by The Advertising Agencies Association of India [AAAI] and The Advertising Club [TAC], they showcase and celebrate the best of the best. There's a dedicated category for Branded Content now which is hotter than a Bollywood dance floor.

And, finally, I'd recommend following some interesting creators who do Branded Content really well. Internationally, Ryan Reynolds; in India, Aiyyo Shraddha, Tanmay Bhat. But explore and learn.

So, there you have it. A galaxy of resources that can build on your branded content. Remember, keep learning, keep telling stories, and keep building your brand's story.

BRANDED CONTENT BRIEF TEMPLATE		
Sr.	**Content**	**Details**
1.	*Client name	
2.	*Brand name	
3.	*Product/ service category	
4.	*Product details	
5.	*Link to brand's communication – latest and legacy	
6.	*Link to social media pages/ handles	
7.	*Tagline	
8.	*Brand ambassadors, celebrity associations, mascots, experts, influencers	
9.	*Target audience, profiles, media habits	
10.	*Priority markets	
11.	*Marketing objectives	
12.	*Campaign objectives	
13.	Competition	
14.	*Key messages for this campaign	
15.	*Target timelines	
16.	*Budget range	
17.	Mandatories	
18.	Metrics to measure success	
19.	*Briefing date	
20.	*Expected turnaround date for 1st cut idea, proposal	
21.	Any other info	

Briefed by:	Brief approved by:
Date:	Date:

Brief received by:	Confirmed by:
Date:	Date:

*Mandatory fields to be filled.
Download blank templates to use at
BrandedContentBoss.com/resources

BRANDED CONTENT PROPOSAL TEMPLATE		
Sr.	**Content**	**Details**
1.	*Client name	
2.	*Brand name	
3.	*Background & Brief	
4.	*Title of Property	
5.	*Idea logline	
6.	*Idea details	
7.	Reference/ tone	
8.	Potential talent associated	
9.	*Brand integration	
10.	Marketing, promotions [optional]	
11.	Extension possibilities	
12.	*Timelines	
13.	Deliverables/ Reach	
14.	*Budgets	
15.	*Proposal validity	

Proposal submitted by:	Confirmed by:
Date:	Date:

Proposal received by:	Confirmed by:
Date:	Date:

*Mandatory fields to be filled.
Download blank templates to use at
BrandedContentBoss.com/resources

TIMELINES/ ROADMAP		
Action	**Responsibility**	**Deadline**
Briefing	Brand	
Concept presentation	Creator	
Feedback	Brand	
Concept tweak, with budget presentation	Creator	
Concept, budget finalization	Brand + Creator	
Paperwork, advances	Brand + Creator	
Prep	Creator	
Final presentation with details, pre-execution	Creator	
Execution	Creator	
Post	Creator	
First cut presentation	Creator	
Feedback	Brand	
Tweak and final presentation	Creator	
Finalization	Brand + Creator	
Final deliveries, versions	Creator	
Final payments	Brand	

Download blank templates to use at
BrandedContentBoss.com/resources

BRANDED CONTENT CALENDAR					
Period	Phase 1 PRE	Phase 2 PREP	Phase 3 EXECN	Phase 4 LAUNCH	Phase 5 TRACK
Wk 1					
Wk 2					
Wk 3					
Wk 4					
Wk 5					
Wk 6					
Wk 7					
Wk 8					
Wk 9					
Wk 10					
Wk 11					
Wk 12					
Wk 13					
Wk 14					

Download blank templates to use at BrandedContentBoss.com/resources

BRANDED CONTENT EVALUATION CHECKLIST			
Sr.	**Entertainment**	**Sr.**	**Branding**
1.	Relatability	1.	Idea/ Theme
2.	Novelty	2.	Brand
3.	Conflict	3.	Product/ Service
4	Simplicity	4.	Benefit
5.	Authenticity	5.	Attribute/ Feature
6.	Extendable	6.	Logo/ Brand name/ Tagline
7.	Timely	7.	Fit with Target Audience
8.	Makes me care	8.	Quality of Execution
		9.	Fit with Tone/ Vibe
		10.	Delivery against brief
		11.	Legal, ethical considerations

Download the checklist at
BrandedContentBoss.com/resources

CHECKLIST FOR SURROUND CONTENT ASSETS	
Sr.	**Format of Ancillary Content**
1.	Teaser poster
2.	Teaser promo
3.	Poster[s]
4.	Motion Poster[s]
5.	Trailer
6.	Song [audio]
7.	Music video
8.	Lyric video
9.	Karaoke video
10.	Karaoke audio
11.	Song dubs
12.	Video [language versions]
13.	Behind the Scenes of the Audio/ Song
14.	Behind the Scenes of the Video
15.	Director's commentary
16.	Song remix
17.	Video remix
18.	Song unplugged
19.	Video unplugged
20.	Stills, photos
21.	Memes, GIFs
22.	Song spoof/ parody
23.	Spoof video
24.	Gender flip version of audio
25.	Edits, cutdown promos
26.	Covers with music influencers
27.	Dance influencer covers
28.	Collaborations on audio
29.	Collaborations on video
30.	Live performance of the song
31.	Flashmob
32.	Contest

33.	Contest – filmmakers
34.	Tutorial – dance
35.	Tutorial – how to play [for different instruments]
36.	Tutorial – vocals
37.	Lyric sheet with meaning
38.	User generated content
39.	Launch event
40.	Concert
41.	Trade, business stories, case study, presentation on strategy/ learnings

Download the checklist at
BrandedContentBoss.com/resources

This is a laundry list of possible surround content for a song/ music video as the primary content piece. All of the assets listed may or may not apply depending on what your primary idea is, but it's a good checklist to tap into to see if you can generate more ancillary content.

REFERENCES

Page	Reference	Source
1	BBC News Anchor being zoom-crashed	BBC News
2	Avengers Assemble image	Disney, Marvel
4	Chinese writer's flyer in 1806	Wikipedia, History of Advertising
4	Charles Dickens' book, 'Dickens on Railways'	Publisher, Safe Haven Books
5	First ever soap opera, 'As the World Turns' produced by P&G	CBS TV Network
6	Binaca Geetmala featuring Ameen Sayani	Radio Ceylon
6	Amul first billboard creative	DaCunha Associates
12 13	200 Insignificant Objects experiment and images	www.significantobjects.com
14	Globe paperweight and letter	www.significantobjects.com
15	Liam Neeson in Taken as meme	20th Century Fox
16	Tom Cruise in Cocktail	Touchstone Pictures
17	Coca-Cola Happiness Machine image	Coca-Cola
18	Dove Real Beauty Sketches image	Unilever, Dove
19	Old Spice ad	P&G

20	Red Bull Stratos space jump image	Red Bull
21	BMW The Hire series poster	BMW Films
40	Dumb Ways to Die campaign poster	Melbourne Metro
41	Fevicol Se song thumbnail, Dabangg 2	T-Series
42	MTV Roadies poster	Viacom18
43	Pasoori thumbnail, Coke Studio	Coke Studio Pakistan
44	The Lego Movie poster	Warner Bros.
45	Barbie movie poster	Warner Bros.
46	Kingfisher Swimsuit Calendar image	United Breweries Group
47	Michelin Guide image	Michelin
48	Bournvita Quiz Contest	Mondelez International
49	Victoria's Secret Fashion Show image	Victoria's Secret Co.
51	Liquid Death taste test image	Liquid Death
51	Carlsberg Friendship test thumbnail	The Carlsberg Foundation
52	Disneyland image	Disney
53	Diana Award mall activation image	The Diana Award, YouTube
54	Prime Video logo	Amazon
55	Mother Nature, Apple ad	Apple
56	Amazon StoryBoxes image	Amazon
58	Semi Girebaal image	Viacom18, MTV
59	BSA SLR ad	BSA Hercules
60	Myntra End of Reason sale ad	Myntra
62	Parking Professor game	Games2win

70	Jabra Fan title song	Yash Raj Films
71	Shape of You, Ed Sheeran, classroom instruments	Jimmy Fallon
71	Diljit Dosanjh, Ikk Kudi unplugged	Zee Records
72	Bank Chor trailer spoof	Yash Raj Films, Y-Films
72	Jiya Re, Alaa Wardi version, Jab Tak Hai Jaan	Yash Raj Films
73	Quick Style, Famous Wedding Show	YouTube, Quick Style
73	ScoopWhoop Café	ScoopWhoop
73	Flashmob at London Foodhall	Sacla Stage Shopera
74	Starships, Pitch Perfect cast, Mike Tompkins	Mike Tompkins, YouTube
74	Happy, Pharrell Williams	YouTube
75	The Beauty Inside, Intel and Toshiba	Intel
78	KBC, Amitabh Bachchan image	Sony Ent. TV
79	Ranveer Ching Returns poster	Capital Foods
80	Kyunki Saas Bhi Kabhi Bahu Thi poster	Star Plus
81	Ryan Reynolds The Vasectomy thumbnail	Aviation Gin
82	Unboxing EX30	Volvo
82	Chef Harpal Sokhi	Capital Foods
85	Amazing Spiderman image	Sony Pictures
86	Devil Baby prank image	20th Century Fox
88	Chipotle's The Scarecrow campaign	Chipotle Mexican Grill
89	Seagram's Imperial Blue	Pernod Ricard India

	ad thumbnail	
90	Sex Chat with Pappu and Papa poster	Yash Raj Films, Y-Films
92	Always #LikeAGirl campaign	P&G
92	Ariel Share the Load campaign	P&G
93	Zoo Zoos campaign	Vodafone, Vi
95	Apple, The Greatest campaign image	Apple
96	6-Pack Band poster	Yash Raj Films, Y-Films
98	Apple, The Underdogs campaign image	Apple
99	Blendtec Will it Blend image	Blendtec
101	Rocket Jawaani song thumbnail	Capital Foods
104	Tweet on Surreal and Sleep Owl	Karthik Srinivasan, Twitter/ X
149	Maruti Ertiga campaign	Maruti Suzuki India Pvt. Ltd.
151	Mere Dad ki Maruti poster	Yash Raj Films, Y-Films
152	Mere Dad ki Maruti images	Yash Raj Films, Y-Films
153	Vishal Sikka interview clip	The Economic Times
156	Ching's Desi Chinese pack	Capital Foods
157	Maggi noodles ad image	Nestle
158	Ranveer Singh magazine cover	GQ
160	Ranveer Ching poster, tweet	Capital Foods
162	Rohit Shetty image, press conference	Capital Foods
163	Amitabh Bachchan tweet	Twitter
163	Rahul Welde post	Facebook

164	Brooke Bond Red Label tea ad	Unilever
166	Hrithik Roshan with the 6-Pack Band	Yash Raj Films, Y-Films
168	Shahrukh Khan with the 6-Pack Band	Yash Raj Films, Y-Films
169	Sheryl Sandberg post	Facebook
194	Airtel 5G sketch by Ashish Chanchlani	YouTube Shorts
203	Dove Thumb-stopping beauty biases	Mindshare
204	Boost Game Stamina Ka screenshots	Mindshare
206	Vim Black images	Mindshare
207	Cric Exchange game integrations	Mindshare
220	Permanent Roommates poster	TVF
225	Yeh Meri Family and Tripling posters	TVF
268	Author image	Ashiish V Patil
Across	All other memes, book cover	Fayyaz Badruddin

ABOUT THE AUTHOR: ASHIISH V PATIL

#HumbleBrag alert:

Ashiish V Patil has been in the game for over three decades, which is probably longer than you've had your favorite old sneakers. Dabbling in Advertising, Marketing, Creative & Content and even handling P&Ls, but what sets him apart is the knack for balancing both the Business AND Creative side of things which gives him the amazing ability to create a harmonious blend of Entertainment and Branding.

Oh boy, the places he's been and the things he's seen. It's like a DJ of the entertainment industry, mixing and mashing up Print to Radio to TV and then boom, having the honor of heading up MTV India! That's right, riding the waves of TV, events, short-form content, music, music videos – you name it, he's done it. And then, he took a leap into Bollywood with Yash Raj Films, to set up a Youth Films vertical, heading their Original Digital Content, Talent Management and Brand Partnerships.

He's a genre-hopping champion with content spanning romance, comedy, thrillers, fiction, non-fiction, travel, quizzes across formats. Including a Children's Book. Over 150 people have made their debuts under his wing – actors, directors, writers, composers, cinematographers, choreographers and as Head of YRF Talent worked with superstar actors, producers and directors.

Now, let me tell you, Ashiish doesn't just talk the talk – he walks the walk. He's a doer. He's worn multiple hats as a writer, producer, director, author, and yes, even a lyricist. He's delivered projects that include series, films, songs that are benchmark case studies, along with a few flops because, hey, that's where the real lessons are learned.

He's worked across diverse categories like FMCG, Consumer Durables, Automobiles, Beverages, Packaged Food, Financial Services, Banks, Pharma, Tourism, Govt. Sector, and non-profits. He's collaborated with blue-chip global brands like Pepsi, Coke, Red

Bull, Puma, BMW, Durex, Unilever to home-grown rockstars and start-ups like Maruti, Ching's Desi Chinese, Red FM, and more. Ashiish brought in India's 1st Cannes Grand Prix Glass Lion with India's 1st Transgender Band that he created for Unilever, 'the 6-Pack Band'; produced India's 1st Branded Feature Film, 'Mere Dad ki Maruti' which is considered the gold standard in Branded Content and was on the AdAge Global Top 50 Creative List of People who mattered.

Ashiish believes the best way to learn is to teach. And he's clocked hours and hours training large teams across functions. He's conducted workshops, spoken at conferences for brands like Google, Viacom, Coca-Cola, PepsiCo, ITC, Lintas, Unilever, Marico, the Future Group, MX Player, Red FM, Leo Burnett, GroupM, the Omnicom Media Group, IIM Kolkata, MICA, ISB, and more. Plus, he's mentored countless creators, and teams across functions.

Ashiish V Patil is one of the earliest proponents of Branded Content before Branded Content was even a thing. He's a lover of storytelling, and if you invite him to your party, he'll bring knowledge, stories, and good vibes. Because at the end of the day, it's not just about the work – it's about enjoying the ride.